T0343845

NEW Close-up English in Use

B1+

Philip James

Additional material: Helen Kidd

NATIONAL
GEOGRAPHIC
LEARNING

Australia • Brazil • Canada • Mexico • Singapore • United Kingdom • United States

Contents

Unit	Grammar	Vocabulary and Use of English
1 pages 4–8	present simple and present continuous	collocations and expressions; exam practice; writing
2 pages 9–13	articles	prepositions; exam practice; writing
3 pages 14–18	past simple and past continuous	phrasal verbs; exam practice; writing
4 pages 19–23	*used to, would, be used to, get used to*	word formation; exam practice; writing
Review 1 pages 24–27	Grammar Exam practice: cloze, open cloze, Grammar and Vocabulary	
5 pages 28–32	present perfect simple and present perfect continuous; *for, since, lately, already, yet* and *still*	prepositions; exam practice; writing
6 pages 33–37	countable and uncountable nouns; quantifiers	collocations and expressions; exam practice; writing
7 pages 38–42	*will* and *be going to*; time expressions	word formation; exam practice; writing
8 pages 43–47	future continuous; future perfect simple	phrasal verbs; exam practice; writing
Review 2 pages 48–51	Grammar Exam practice: word formation, cloze, Grammar and Vocabulary	
9 pages 52–56	modals and semi-modals	prepositions; exam practice; writing
10 pages 57–61	perfect modals	collocations and expressions; exam practice; writing
11 pages 62–66	past perfect simple and past perfect continuous	phrasal verbs; exam practice; writing
12 pages 67–71	question tags; reflexive, indefinite and possessive pronouns	word formation; exam practice; writing
Review 3 pages 72–75	Grammar Exam practice: open cloze, word formation, Grammar and Vocabulary	

Unit	Grammar	Vocabulary and Use of English
13 pages 76–80	*-ing* form; infinitives	collocations and expressions; exam practice; writing
14 pages 81–85	comparison of adjectives and adverbs; *too, enough, so* and *such*	prepositions; exam practice; writing
15 pages 86–90	the passive	phrasal verbs; exam practice; writing
16 pages 91–95	the passive: *-ing* form, infinitives and modal verbs, impersonal and personal structures	word formation; exam practice; writing
Review 4 pages 96–99	Grammar Exam practice: cloze, open cloze, Grammar and Vocabulary	
17 pages 100–105	reported speech: statements; changes in time and place; reported questions	collocations and expressions; exam practice; writing
18 pages 106–110	reported speech: commands and requests; reporting verbs	prepositions; exam practice; writing
19 pages 111–115	conditionals: zero, first, second, third and mixed	word formation; exam practice; writing
20 pages 116–119	conditionals without *if*; *wish* and *if only*	phrasal verbs; exam practice; writing
Review 5 pages 120–123	Grammar Exam practice: word formation, cloze, Grammar and Vocabulary	
21 pages 124–127	relative clauses: defining and non-defining	collocations and expressions; exam practice; writing
22 pages 128–131	reduced relative clauses	prepositions; exam practice; writing
23 pages 132–135	causative	phrasal verbs; exam practice; writing
24 pages 136–140	Inversion: *never, under no circumstances* and *not only … but also*; *It's (about / high) time*	word formation; exam practice; writing
Review 6 pages 141–144	Grammar Exam practice: open cloze, word formation, Grammar and Vocabulary	

Unit 1

Awareness

1 Which of these sentences are correct (C) and incorrect (I)?

1   Jenny live in a big house. ___
2   We usually work on Saturday mornings. ___
3   What colour is Tom paint his bedroom? ___
4   The kids are danceing in the garden. ___
5   I once a week go to the gym. ___

6   Are you coming to dinner tonight? ___
7   I don't watch often TV. ___
8   Why is she always asking you for money? ___
9   No, I not going out tomorrow night. ___
10 We're having a party next weekend. ___

How many did you get right? ☐

Grammar

Present simple

Affirmative	Negative	Questions
I / We / You / They work. He / She / It works.	I / We / You /they **don't** work. He / She / It **doesn't** work.	**Do** I / we / you / they work? **Does** he / she / it work?
Short Answers		
Yes, I / we / you / they do. **Yes**, he / she / it **does**.	**No**, I / we / you / they **don't**. **No**, he / she / it **doesn't**.	

We use the present simple for:

• facts and general truths.
*Apples **grow** on apple trees.*

• routines and habits (often with adverbs of frequency).
*I **often wear** a hat in the summer.*

• permanent states.
Maria lives in a big flat in Madrid.

• timetabled events in the future.
*Our train **arrives** at 7.45 tomorrow morning.*

• story narratives, jokes and sports commentaries.
*Zoe **passes** the ball to Lucy and Lucy scores!*

Note

Some common time expressions that are often used with the present simple are *every day / week / month / winter, every other day, once a week, twice a month, at the weekend, in April, in the morning / afternoon / evening, at night, on Thursdays, on Saturday mornings*, etc.
*They go to the south of France **every summer**.*

Remember

We often use adverbs of frequency with the present simple. They tell us how often something happens.
They come before the main verb, but after the verb *be*.
*Tom is **rarely** late for football training.*   *We **always** watch TV in the evenings.*
Some common adverbs of frequency are: *always, usually, often, sometimes, rarely / hardly ever / seldom, never.*

Present continuous

Affirmative	Negative	Questions
I **am** (**'m**) play**ing**. He / she / it **is** (**'s**) play**ing**. We / You / They **are** (**'re**) play**ing**.	I **am** (**'m**) **not** play**ing**. He / She / it **is not** (**isn't**) play**ing**. We / You / They **are not** (**aren't**) play**ing**.	**Am** I play**ing**? **Is** he / she / it play**ing**? **Are** we / you / they play**ing**?
Short Answers		
Yes, I **am**. Yes, he / she / it **is**. Yes, we / you / they **are**.	**No**, I'm **not**. **No**, he / she / it **isn't**. **No**, we / you / they **aren't**.	

Spelling: dance → danc**ing**, travel → trave**lling**, tidy → ti**dying**

We use the present continuous for:

- actions that are in progress at or around the time of speaking.
I'm doing my homework.
- temporary situations.
Simon is staying with his aunt at the moment.
- situations that are changing or developing in the present.
Exams are getting more difficult.
- an annoying habit (often with *always, continually, constantly* and *forever*).
You are always trying to play tricks on me!
- what is happening in a picture.
Some people are lying on the beach. A child is playing with a dog.
- fixed plans and arrangements for the future.
They are going on holiday next month.

Note

Some common time expressions that are often used with the present continuous are *at the moment, now, for the time being, this morning / afternoon / evening / week / month / year, today,* etc.
*Ana is staying with a friend **for the time being**.*

Stative verbs

Some verbs are not usually used in continuous tenses. They are called *stative verbs* because they describe states and not actions. To talk about the present, we use these verbs in the present simple tense. These are the most common:

- verbs of emotion: *hate, like, love, need, prefer, want.*
I hate the colour brown.
- verbs of senses: *feel, hear, see, smell, sound, taste.*
This coffee smells great.
- verbs expressing a state of mind: *believe, doubt, forget, imagine, know, remember, seem, suppose, think, understand.*
I imagine she lives in a beautiful house.
- verbs of possession: *belong to, have, own, possess.*
My uncle owns this shop.
- other verbs: *be, consist, contain, cost, include, mean.*
How much does this jacket cost?

Some verbs can be both stative verbs and action verbs, but with a different meaning. These are the most common:

be	Sam **is** very well behaved. (usual behaviour) He**'s being** very naughty just now. (at the moment; not their normal behaviour)
expect	I **expect** she is very pleased with her results. (expect = think or believe) We**'re expecting** rain this weekend. (expect = wait for)
have	Susan **has (got)** five brothers. (have = own / possess) They**'re having** a fantastic time at summer camp. (have = experience) I'm **having coffee** with my cousin tomorrow. (have = eat / drink)
look	She **looks** like a film star. (look like = resembles) I'm **looking** for a new laptop. (look for = search)
taste	This milk **tastes** bad. (taste = have a particular flavour) The chef **is tasting** the soup. (taste = test the flavour)
think	He **thinks** he's a great singer. (think = have an opinion) They**'re thinking** of selling their car. (think = consider)
see	I **see** what you mean now! (see = understand) I'm **seeing** the doctor this afternoon. (see = meet)
smell	Dinner **smells** delicious! (smell = have a particular smell) Why **are** you **smelling** your socks? (smell = action of smelling)
weigh	Dan **weighs** 58 kg. (weigh = have a particular weight) Tom **is weighing** the flour. (weigh = measure the weight)

Note

We can use both *have* and *have got* for possession. The meaning is the same, but *have got* is more informal. We can't use *have got* as an action verb.

1

Grammar exercises

2 **Choose the correct option to complete the sentences.**

1 Tanya always *reads / is reading* the sports news first.
2 My *parents have / are having* dinner at an expensive restaurant tonight.
3 I *don't watch / 'm not watching* romantic films.
4 We *go / are going* to the theatre once a month.
5 Gabe *stays / is staying* in bed for the time being.
6 I hardly ever *wear / am wearing* shoes in the house.
7 How *do you get / are you getting* to school every day?
8 Can you be quiet please? I *try / am trying* to do some work.
9 What *do you do / are you doing* at the moment?
10 *Does she come / Is she coming* out with us on Friday?

3 **Complete the sentences with the present simple or present continuous form of the verbs.**

1 The children _____ (play) in the front room at the moment.
2 I _____ (have) dinner at my friend's house tomorrow evening.
3 Light _____ (travel) at 186,000 miles per second.
4 Mr James _____ (teach) us maths on Wednesdays.
5 She _____ (always / try) to get better marks than me at school. It's so annoying!
6 We _____ (go) to Italy every winter.
7 The last performance _____ (start) at eleven o'clock.
8 I _____ (not eat) anything at the moment because I _____ (feel) ill.

4 **Choose the correct option (a–c) to complete the sentences.**

1 Sandra is working on her project ___ .
   a usually   **b** now   **c** hardly ever

2 We spend a lot of time at the beach ___ .
   a every summer   **b** this summer   **c** next summer

3 ___ I have time to practise the guitar.
   a this morning   **b** once a week   **c** rarely

4 Why are you ___ arguing with me?
   a always   **b** today   **c** seldom

5 Sorry, madam. We don't have any tomato soup ___ .
   a never   **b** every day   **c** this evening

6 The Barkers are going camping ___ .
   a constantly   **b** next weekend   **c** twice a month

5 **Match the questions (1–8) with their answers (a–h).**

1 What are you drinking at the moment?   [ ]   **a** Coffee.
2 Do your grandparents live in a big flat?   [ ]   **b** No, I'm not.
3 Is it a beautiful day today?   [ ]   **c** Yes, she does.
4 How often do you go swimming?   [ ]   **d** Canada.
5 Are the children sleeping on the floor?   [ ]   **e** Yes, it is.
6 Does your aunt drive a bus?   [ ]   **f** Every week.
7 Are you worrying about the exams?   [ ]   **g** Yes, they are.
8 Where are you going on holiday this year?   [ ]   **h** No, they don't.

6 Complete the sentences with the present simple or present continuous form of the verbs.

1 **expect**
   a I _____ you'll be hungry by the time you get home tonight.
   b We _____ a letter from the head teacher this week.

2 **have**
   a Your car _____ a flat tyre.
   b Where _____ (we) lunch this afternoon?

3 **think**
   a Izzy _____ of going to cookery classes.
   b What _____ (you) of the latest Marvel comic movie?

4 **see**
   a She _____ her boyfriend at seven o'clock this evening.
   b I hope you _____ what I mean now.

7 Write questions using the present simple or present continuous form of the verbs.

1 you / eat / in a restaurant / every week?
   Do you eat in a restaurant every week?

2 what time / Jen / usually / come home?

3 you / do / your homework at the moment?

4 why / the little boy / cry?

5 who / you / usually / go / to the cinema with?

6 she / think / of moving to a new house?

Vocabulary

Collocations and expressions

8 Match the expressions (1–8) with their meanings (a–h).

1 be a natural   a look forward to something
2 be dying to   b have the same interests
3 be mad about   c continue to be in contact with someone
4 fall out with   d spend time with someone
5 keep in touch with   e like or love something very much
6 get on someone's nerves   f annoy someone
7 hang out   g be extremely good at
8 have a lot in common h have an argument with someone

9 Complete the sentences with these words.

black   blue   colours   gold   green   red

1 I love babysitting for the Andersons because the children are as good as _____ .
2 Mum has given us the _____ light to plan a surprise party for Dad.

3 Our science teacher saw _____ when a few students didn't tidy up after the experiment.

4 I thought he was always calm, but he showed his true _____ when he got angry with us.

5 When he's feeling a bit _____ he likes to go to the cinema to cheer himself up.

6 It's a confusing situation – it isn't exactly _____ and white.

Exam practice

Sentence transformation

10 **Complete the second sentence so that it has a similar meaning to the first sentence, using the word given. Do not change the word given. You must use between two and five words.**

1 Simon really resembles his father.

Simon really _____ his father.   **LIKE**

2 My brother complains about my music all the time.

My brother is _____ about my music.   **CONTINUALLY**

3 We seldom go camping without our dog.

We _____ without our dog.   **OFTEN**

4 I go to karate classes every Wednesday and Friday with my cousin.

I go to karate classes _____ with my cousin.   **TWICE**

5 Jake nearly always stays in bed until after 8 a.m.

Jake _____ before 8 a.m.   **HARDLY**

6 My new bike is very light.

My new bike _____ very much.   **WEIGH**

7 The departure time of our flight is 22.45.

Our flight _____ 22.45.   **AT**

8 We have an appointment to see the head teacher this afternoon.

We _____ this afternoon.   **ARE**

Word formation

11 **Use the word in capitals to form a word that fits in the gap.**

1 Lucy writes beautiful stories – they're always full of such _____ ideas.   **IMAGINE**

2 Our teacher has a lot of energy and _____ .   **ENTHUSE**

3 You should ask David to do it if it's important – he's very _____ .   **SENSE**

4 I felt quite anxious and _____ before my piano exam.   **STRESS**

5 She's a very popular and _____ person.   **ATTRACT**

6 We love going to our villa in the countryside – it's so quiet and _____ .   **PEACE**

7 Young people can suffer from _____ as well as old people.   **LONELY**

8 He has a great _____ , but he doesn't have enough qualifications for the job.   **PERSON**

Writing

12 **Write a paragraph in your notebook about a good friend or a family member. Write about what they are like, what they like and don't like, and what you like doing together.**

Awareness

1 Which of these sentences are correct (C) and incorrect (I)?

1 Mr Stevens is doctor. ___
2 I'll see you in an hour. ___
3 The sun is bright today! ___
4 We took a trip down Thames in the London. ___
5 I'm learning to play the piano. ___
6 Do you speak the French? ___
7 My dad is great songwriter. ___
8 You're the funniest person I know. ___
9 Have you ever been to the Australia? ___
10 He travelled the world by motorcycle. ___

How many did you get right? ☐

Grammar

The indefinite article: *a / an*

We use *a* before a consonant sound.

a chemist   *a* university

We use *an* before a vowel sound.

an actor   *an* hour   *an* X-ray   *an* MA degree

We use *a / an*:
* with singular countable nouns.
*Could I have **an** apple, please?*
* to mean *per / each* in expressions of frequency.
*I go swimming three times **a** week.*
* to mention something for the first time. (When we continue talking about it we use *the*.)
*I've got **a** new bike. **The** bike has 18 gears.*
* to show job, status, etc.
*She's **a** famous scientist.*

The definite article: *the*

We use *the* with singular and plural countable nouns and uncountable nouns to talk about something specific when the noun is mentioned for a second time.
*At last, there's **a** bus! Oh no, **the** bus isn't stopping.*

We also use *the* before:

* unique nouns.
***The** sun is at the centre of **the** solar system.*
* names of cinemas, theatres, ships, hotels, etc.
*We're going to **the** New Theatre tonight.*
*How much is a room in **the** Grand Hotel?*
* names of rivers, deserts, mountain ranges, and names or nouns with *of*.
*Where are **the** Himalayas?*
*Have you seen **the** Tower of Pisa?*
* countries or groups of countries whose names are plural.
*She was born in **the** Philippines.*
*We went to **the** United States last year.*
* musical instruments.
*Do you play **the** violin?*
* nationalities.
***The** Ancient Greeks loved sport.*

- adjectives used as nouns.

*Do you think we should do more to help **the** jobless?*

- superlatives.

*She's **the** fastest runner in my school.*

- the words *beach, countryside, station, jungle*, etc.

*How would you survive in **the** jungle?*

- the words *morning, afternoon, evening*.

*I hate getting up in **the** morning.*

We do not use *the* before:

- proper nouns.

David *is in* **Spain**.

- subjects of study.

*Do you prefer **history** or **geography**?*

- names of countries, cities, streets (BUT: *the high street*), squares, bridges (BUT: *the Golden Gate Bridge*), parks, stations, individual mountains, islands, lakes, continents.

Waterloo Station, *in* **London**, *is close to* **Waterloo Bridge**.

Aconcagua *is the highest mountain in* **South America**.

- *bed, school, hospital, prison, university, college, court* when we talk about something related to the main purpose of the place. (*Work* never takes *the*.)

*Jake is in **hospital**.* (He is ill.)

*Jake's mum has gone to **the hospital** to visit him.* (Jake's mum is not ill; she's gone to visit Jake.)

- means of transport in expressions like *by car*, etc. (BUT: *in the car*).

*We travelled round the city by **bike**.*

- names of sports, games, colours, days, months, drinks, holidays, meals, and languages (not followed by the word *language*).

*My sister's football team wears **blue**.*

*Ana speaks **Spanish**, **Portuguese** and **Italian**.*

*What did you eat for **lunch** on Saturday?*

> **Note**
>
> When we refer specifically to a meal, a drink, etc. we use *the*.
> **The breakfast** *at the hotel was expensive.*
> **The coffee** *here is always delicious.*

Grammar exercises

2 Choose the correct option to complete the sentences.

1 I have a driving lesson once *the / a / –* week.
2 It's dangerous to go swimming when *the / a / –* sea is so rough.
3 She travelled round Europe by *the / a / –* train last summer.
4 Uncle Sam is *the / an / –* expert rock climber.
5 I hope Portugal wins *the / a / –* World Cup.
6 Oh no! We've got *the / a / –* biology this afternoon.
7 He's always tired when he gets home from *the / a / –* work in *the / an / –* evening.
8 Did you know there's *the / a / –* new café on *the / a / –* high street?

3 Complete the sentences with *the* or – (no article).

1 Have you ever seen _____ Eiffel Tower?
2 I forgot to eat _____ breakfast this morning!
3 I think I left my keys in _____ car.
4 My cousin is studying _____ art at _____ college.
5 She moved to _____ countryside when she retired.
6 We didn't enjoy _____ soup last night, but _____ dessert was delicious.
7 What's _____ best present you've ever had for _____ Christmas?
8 The kids are playing _____ basketball in _____ garden.

4 Complete the sentences with *a*, *an*, *the* or – (no article).

1 Have you read _____ book I lent you?
2 There was _____ strange light in _____ sky last night.
3 She's studying in _____ Germany, but she doesn't speak _____ German.
4 Only Mark made _____ useful contribution to _____ discussion.
5 Is _____ badminton _____ easy sport to play?
6 Some people think _____ life of _____ teacher is _____ easy one.
7 Nearly everyone believes that _____ peace is preferable to _____ war.
8 When I was at _____ school, my favourite subject was _____ geography because I enjoyed learning about continents like _____ Asia.

5 Complete the conversation with *a*, *an*, *the* or – (no article).

Sam: It was my birthday on ¹ _____ Sunday.

Julia: Did you have ² _____ party?

Sam: No, ³ _____ party was cancelled.

Julia: That's ⁴ _____ pity. Was it cancelled because of ⁵ _____ weather?

Sam: Yes. I wanted ⁶ _____ barbecue in ⁷ _____ garden, but it was too rainy.

Julia: I hope you had ⁸ _____ fun anyway. What presents did you get?

Sam: I got ⁹ _____ bike and ¹⁰ _____ electric guitar.

Julia: I didn't know you played ¹¹ _____ guitar.

Sam: I don't. I'm starting ¹² _____ lessons next week at ¹³ _____ music school next to ¹⁴ _____ Manor Park.

Julia: That's a long way from ¹⁵ _____ home, isn't it?

Sam: Yes, it is. That's what ¹⁶ _____ new bike is for.

6 Complete the text with *a*, *an*, *the* or – (no article).

Hi Ella

How are you feeling? It's ¹ _____ shame you missed ² _____ school today because it was ³ _____ most interesting day of ⁴ _____ year so far! We have ⁵ _____ new student in our class. His name is Mark and he's from ⁶ _____ USA. ⁷ _____ teacher told me to look after him and show him around ⁸ _____ school! He's ⁹ _____ really nice person. We had ¹⁰ _____ lunch together in the canteen and he told me all about ¹¹ _____ life in ¹² _____ America.

Mark's dad is ¹³ _____ accountant, which is funny because Mark hates ¹⁴ _____ maths! In fact, he prefers ¹⁵ _____ sport to any other school subject. He told me he was ¹⁶ _____ best tennis player in his school – and he's only 13. I asked him if he was good at ¹⁷ _____ football, and he said yes – but then we realised we were talking about ¹⁸ _____ different game! ¹⁹ _____ Americans call it ²⁰ _____ 'soccer' – and he doesn't like that game at all.

Get well soon.

Maria

7 Correct the mistakes in these sentences.

1 I've got a great news for you.
  Do you eat in a restaurant every week? _____

2 Amazon is a very long river.
  _____

3 Do you speak the Portuguese?
  _____

4 What are we having for the dinner?
  _____

5 Greta is going to the college next year.
  _____

6 This is an unique opportunity for me.
  _____

7 Greg is rich businessman.
  _____

8 I never learned to play a piano.
  _____

9 We went to the top of an Empire State Building in New York.
  _____

10 What did you have for the breakfast?
  _____

Vocabulary

Prepositions

8 Complete the phrases with these prepositions. Some prepositions can be used more than once.

about	at	for	in	of	on

1 approve _____   5 nervous _____
2 _____ fun   6 sense _____ humour
3 _____ my spare time   7 shout _____
4 laugh _____   8 spend money _____

9 Complete the sentences with the phrases from Exercise 8.

1 Kate's jokes are really funny. She's got a great _____ .
2 There are lots of things I enjoy doing outside of work, _____ .
3 Are you really serious about playing the piano, or is it something you just do _____ ?
4 Mo was feeling very _____ his science exam, but he got a good mark.
5 Please don't _____ me – I can hear you perfectly clearly when you talk in a normal voice.
6 Do you _____ clothes every week or do you prefer to save?
7 I didn't _____ the joke because I didn't think it was funny.
8 Her parents don't _____ her new friend. They don't think she's very caring.

Exam practice

Sentence transformation

10 Complete the second sentence so that it has a similar meaning to the first sentence, using the word given. Do not change the word given. You must use between two and five words.

1 Sam has gone to Italy to learn the language.
Sam is _____ Italy.

ITALIAN

2 I love music, but my neighbour's loud music really annoys me.
I love music, but my neighbour's loud music really _____ .

NERVES

3 The children were very well-behaved in the cinema.
The children _____ in the cinema.

GOLD

4 My aunt teaches engineering at the local college.
My aunt _____ at the local college.

TEACHER

5 We went to dance classes on Mondays and Wednesdays when we were children.
We went to dance classes _____ when we were children.

TWICE

6 Danny is a really good guitarist.
Danny _____ very well.

GUITAR

7 No one in our school swims faster than me.
I _____ in our school.

FASTEST

8 The basketball team my brother plays for has a red uniform.
My brother's _____ a red uniform.

WEARS

Word formation

11 Use the word in capitals to form a word that fits in the gap.

1 Sarah is successful because she has a lot of _____ .

CONFIDENT

2 You'll be a great nurse – you're a very _____ person.

CARE

3 I felt very _____ when I had to collect my medal in front of everyone.

EMBARRASS

4 I used to be very good at _____ when I was younger.

GYMNAST

5 How many times has your team won the _____ ?

CHAMPION

6 He's fun to be with because he's always so _____ .

CHEER

7 Some people are _____ good at sports.

NATURE

8 The government needs to spend more money on _____ .

EDUCATE

Writing

12 Read the writing task and write your answer in 140–190 words in an appropriate style.

You have received an email from an English-speaking friend. One of his friends, Dan, is coming to your town. Your friend would like you to spend an afternoon with Dan to show him your town. Write an email to Dan telling him about:

- yourself, your family and your likes and dislikes
- some places in your town that you would recommend to a visitor.

Unit 3

Awareness

1 Which of these sentences are correct (C) and incorrect (I)?

1 I read a lot of books last year. ___
2 We didn't walked home. ___
3 She got up early on the morning. ___
4 They were watching TV at eight o'clock. ___
5 The dog didn't wanting a bath. ___
6 He was riding a horse when he felled. ___
7 Were you studying all day? ___
8 Did all the students passed the test? ___
9 They didn't go out last night. ___
10 I wasn't feeling well that morning. ___

How many did you get right? ☐

Grammar

Past simple

Affirmative	Negative	Questions
I / He / She / It / We / You / They work**ed**.	I / He / She / It / We / You / They **didn't** work.	**Did** I / he / she / it / we / you / they work?
Short Answers		
Yes, I / he /she / it / we / you / they **did**.	**No**, I / he / she / it / we / you / they **didn't**.	

Spelling: dance → danc**ed**, travel → trave**lled**, study → stud**ied**, stay → stay**ed**

We use the past simple for:
* something that started and finished in the past.
*He **studied** geology at university.*
* past routines and habits (often with adverbs of frequency).
*Katy often **climbed** trees when she was little.*
* actions that happened one after the other in the past, for example when telling a story.
*They **went** into the cave and **heard** a strange noise.*

> **Note**
> Some verbs are irregular and do not follow these spelling rules. See a list of irregular verbs on pages 145–146.

> **Note**
> Some common time expressions that are often used with the past simple are *yesterday, last night / week / month / summer, a week / month / year ago, twice a week, once a month, at the weekend, in July, in the morning / afternoon / evening, at night, on Sundays, on Friday mornings*, etc.
> *I listened to some great new bands **at the weekend**.*

Past continuous

Affirmative	Negative	Questions
I / He / she / It **was** work**ing**. We / You / They **were** work**ing**.	I / He / She / It **was not** (**wasn't**) working We / You / They **were not** (**weren't**) working.	**Was** I / he / she / it work**ing**? **Were** we / you / they work**ing**?
Short Answers		
Yes, I / he / she / it **was**. **Yes**, we / you / they **were**.	**No**, I / he / she / it **wasn't**. **No**, we / you / they **weren't**.	

Spelling: write → writ**ing**, travel → trave**lling**, study → study**ing**

We use the past continuous for

- actions that were in progress at a specific time in the past.
*We **were playing** chess at nine o'clock last night.*

- two or more past actions in progress at the same time.
*They **were watching** TV while the baby **was sleeping**.*

- giving background information in a story.
*The sun **was shining** and people **were sitting** in the shade.*

- an action in progress in the past that was interrupted by another action.
*Max **was cooking** dinner when his phone **rang**.*

Note

Some common time expressions that are often used with the past continuous are *while, as, all day / week / month / year, at ten o'clock last night, last Monday / week / year, this morning,* etc.
*They were learning about the Romans **this morning**.*

Grammar exercises

2 **Choose the correct option to complete the sentences.**

1 I *walked / was walking* the dog when it started to rain.

2 *Did / Were* you see that shooting star?

3 That *wasn't / wasn't being* a very funny joke.

4 The audience *clapped / was clapping* when the performance ended.

5 *Did you work / Were you working* when the teacher came in the room?

6 How many children *did you take / were you taking* to the park yesterday?

7 We *didn't get / weren't getting* any tickets because they were too expensive.

8 He *went / was going* downstairs and *ran / was running* out of the door.

9 While I *slept / was sleeping* a bird *flew / was flying* through the window.

10 It *rained / was raining* when I *left / was leaving* school this afternoon.

3 **Complete the sentences with the past simple or past continuous form of the verbs.**

1 We _____ (discover) a new café in the city last night.

2 Sammy _____ (tidy) his room when his mum _____ (come) in.

3 They _____ (go) to the bookshop and _____ (bought) a book about Peru.

4 I _____ (text) while the teacher _____ (talk).

5 Martha _____ (hear) a noise outside her tent, so she _____ (shout) for help.

6 _____ (you / see) the programme about unusual weather last night?

7 What book _____ (John / read) when you _____ (meet) him?

8 She _____ (hurt) herself while she _____ (decorate) the garage.

3

4 Match the questions (1–10) with their answers (a–j).

1	Were you sleeping?	☐	a	No, I didn't.
2	Did your sister enjoy the film?	☐	b	Because she was sad.
3	Where did they stay?	☐	c	Yes, I was.
4	Were those boys bothering you?	☐	d	Yes, it was.
5	Was it raining when you got home?	☐	e	No, they didn't.
6	What did David say to you?	☐	f	In a hotel.
7	Did those people pay for their tickets?	☐	g	Yes, she did.
8	Did you finish your homework?	☐	h	No, they weren't.
9	Why was she crying?	☐	i	Daniel.
10	Who told you my secret?	☐	j	Nothing.

5 Complete the conversation with the past simple or past continuous form of the verbs.

Mia: Hey, Steve. You'll never guess what I [1] _____ (see) last night.

Zak: What [2] _____ (you / see)?

Mia: A UFO! I [3] _____ (wake) up at about two in the morning, and I [4] _____ (not can) get back to sleep. So I [5] _____ (go) downstairs for some milk.

Zak: What [6] _____ (happen) then?

Mia: I [7] _____ (pour) the milk into a glass when I [8] _____ (hear) a strange noise outside.

Zak: What [9] _____ (you / do) next?

Mia: I [10] _____ (open) the back door, and [11] _____ (look) up into the sky. A large white light [12] _____ (float) above the trees! Then suddenly it [13] _____ (fly) up into the sky and [14] _____ (disappear) behind the clouds.

Zak: [15] _____ (your mum or dad / see) it too?

Mia: No, they [16] _____ (sleep).

Zak: I don't believe you. I think you [17] _____ (dream).

Mia: I [18] _____ (not dream). It actually [19] _____ (happen). I know it [20] _____ (be) real!

6 Complete the questions.

1 **A:** _____ at seven o'clock yesterday morning?
   B: No, I wasn't having breakfast. I was still in bed!

2 **A:** What time _____ ?
   B: I got up at 8.30.

3 **A:** _____ when you went outside?
   B: No, the sun wasn't shining. It was raining.

4 **A:** Why _____ yesterday afternoon?
   B: I went to the library because I needed a quiet place to study.

5 **A:** _____ anyone there?
   B: Yes, I met my friend Jake.

6 **A:** What _____ ?
   B: He was trying to finish an essay.

7 **A:** _____ when he came into the library?
   B: Yes, I was studying.

8 **A:** _____ anywhere interesting after the library?
   B: No, we didn't. We both went home.

7 Complete the sentences with one word in each gap.

1 I _____ working on a project about the Incas last night.

2 _____ you remember to take a photo?

3 Tim was painting his room _____ he fell off the ladder.

4 We ate dinner at six o'clock _____ the evening.

5 _____ the twins playing nicely together when you got home?

6 They weren't watching TV _____ day, were they?

7 My mum was packing up the tent _____ my dad was cooking breakfast.

8 What time _____ they finally arrive?

Vocabulary

Phrasal verbs

8 Match the phrasal verbs (1–8) with their meanings (a–h).

1	be into	☐	a	discover a fact or information
2	come across	☐	b	find an answer or solution to something
3	find out	☐	c	trust or have confidence in someone or something
4	look into	☐	d	manage to see something which is difficult to see
5	make out	☐	e	find something by chance
6	make up	☐	f	try to discover the facts about something
7	rely on	☐	g	be very interested in
8	work out	☐	h	say something that isn't true

9 Complete the sentences with the phrasal verbs from Exercise 8.

1 I don't believe your story. I think you're _____ it _____ .

2 You can always _____ Dan to give his honest opinion.

3 I can hear music, but I can't _____ where it's coming from.

4 If you look closely at the sky, you can just _____ the northern lights.

5 They were playing in the park when they _____ some strange footprints.

6 Did you ever _____ who sent you that text message?

7 I'm going to buy this book for my sister. She _____ really _____ detective stories.

8 Scientists are _____ possible reasons for the unusual weather patterns.

3

Exam practice

Sentence transformation

10 Complete the second sentence so that it has a similar meaning to the first sentence, using the word given. Do not change the word given. You must use between two and five words.

1 We discovered the old photos while we were tidying our room.
   We were tidying our room when we _____ the old photos.   **CAME**

2 During our walk in the woods, we heard a strange noise.
   We _____ when we heard a strange noise.   **WERE**

3 My parents didn't believe me. They thought I was inventing the story.
   My parents didn't believe me. They thought I _____ the story.   **MAKING**

4 How long did it take you to solve question 7?
   How long did it take you to _____ the answer to question 7?   **WORK**

5 When I called, Tom was still asleep.
   Tom _____ I called.   **SLEEPING**

6 After starting the engine, Sally drove away.
   Sally _____ drove away.   **THEN**

7 I was reading and my sister was watching TV at the same time.
   My sister _____ I was reading.   **WHILE**

8 Mike spent last summer reading books about volcanoes.
   Mike _____ of books about volcanoes last summer.   **LOT**

Word formation

11 Use the word in capitals to form a word that fits in the gap.

1 If a place is _____ , that means that there are too many people living there.   **POPULATE**

2 Do you really believe that theory? It seems very _____ to me.   **LIKELY**

3 A local farmer reported the _____ of some unusual lines and shapes in his field.   **APPEAR**

4 The first people to arrive lived in a _____ near the coast.   **SETTLE**

5 There will be an _____ into this tragic accident.   **INVESTIGATE**

6 I woke up to see a _____ light shining in the sky.   **MYSTERY**

7 My brother wants to be an _____ when he finishes university.   **ARCHAEOLOGY**

8 Scientists managed to maintain the _____ of the location.   **SECRET**

Writing

12 Write a paragraph in your notebook. Write about what you and your family were doing at eight o'clock last night. What did you do after that?

Unit 4

Awareness

1 Which of these sentences are correct (C) and incorrect (I)?

1 He used to travel to some amazing places for work. ___

2 I would love swimming when I was a child. ___

3 Did you use to live in France? ___

4 They would go skiing every weekend. ___

5 I'm not used to this new app yet. ___

6 You'll get used to it soon. ___

7 Mark didn't use to like carrots. ___

8 I was used to getting up early very quickly. ___

9 She thought she would never used to the heat. ___

10 We use to study French at our old school. ___

How many did you get right? ☐

Grammar

used to and *would*

We use *used to* + infinitive for:

• actions we did regularly in the past, but not now.
*She **used to play** the violin when she was young.*

• states that existed in the past, but that don't exist now.
*He **used to like** driving, but now he prefers cycling.*

We use *would* + infinitive for actions that we did regularly in the past, but not now. We don't use it for past states.
*We **would go** to the beach every day when we lived in Australia.*

be used to and *get used to*

We use *be used to* + -*ing* form / noun to talk about something that is usual or familiar.
*Andy is **used to working at night** because he's a nurse.*
*Jo is used to **physical work** because she grew up on a farm.*

We use *get used to* + -*ing* form / noun to talk about actions and states which are becoming more familiar.
*I'm slowly **getting used to the idea** of living in a flat.*

> **Note**
>
> *Be* and *get* change depending on the tense that is needed in the context.
> *She's **used to fixing** engines. She's had lots of experience.*
> *He **has been getting used to** his new design software.*

Grammar exercises

2 Choose the correct option to complete the sentences.

1 When I was a baby I *used to / would* love bananas and chocolate sauce.

2 She isn't used to *live / working* outdoors all day.

3 We would *eat / eating* fish for dinner every Friday evening.

4 The museum *used to / would* be closed on Mondays.

5 He *would / were used* to spend hours reading about the Aztecs and the Maya.

6 Don't worry, you'll soon *be / get* used to sleeping in a tent.

7 I *would / used to* speak Portuguese, but I can't anymore.

8 He *wouldn't / wasn't used* to stay up after ten o'clock when he was a boy.

9 She isn't nervous because she *is used to / gets used* to giving presentations.

10 It took me a long time to *be / get* used to living in such a big city.

3 How did people live 200 years ago? Complete the sentences with *used to* or *didn't use to*.

1 They _____ travel by plane.

2 They _____ travel by horse.

3 They _____ write emails.

4 They _____ write letters.

5 Children _____ work in factories.

6 They _____ live as long as we do.

7 They _____ have telephones.

8 They _____ have cleaner air than we have now.

4 Write the questions for the interview.

1 where / play?

Where did you use to play? _____

I used to play in the street with my friends.

2 how / get to school?

_____

I used to walk.

3 have / lots of friends?

_____

Yes, I did.

4 go abroad on holiday?

_____

No, I never went abroad.

5 your family / have a car?

_____

Yes, we did.

6 enjoy / school?

_____

No, I never liked it.

7 what subject / be good at?

_____

I used to be good at maths.

8 get into trouble at school?

_____

No, I was a good boy!

5 Complete the sentences with *be used to* or *get used to*.

1 I (not) _____ working at weekends.

2 He says he'll never _____ driving an automatic car.

3 We _____ getting lots of homework at this school.

4 My friends (not) _____ seeing me with short hair.

5 It was hard at first, but he soon _____ getting up at 5 a.m.

6 I don't mind having dinner late in the evening – I _____ it.

7 When she first arrived in England, she (not) _____ taking an umbrella with her everywhere.

8 She soon _____ the rainy weather!

6 Read about the situations and complete the sentences with *used to*.

1 You have to wear a uniform at your new school.
You'll *have to get used to wearing a uniform* _____ .

2 The Smiths moved from the country to the city. It's much noisier there.
They weren't _____ .

3 The children found life very different in the city, but it wasn't a problem for them.
The children soon _____ .

4 You usually go to bed before 10 p.m., but last night you stayed up till midnight, so today you're very tired.
You _____ .

5 Grandad has a new smartphone. He finds it difficult to use.
Grandad doesn't think he'll ever _____ .

6 Tom lives in Ecuador. At first, he didn't like the hot weather, but he's OK now.
Tom _____ .

7 Complete the sentences with one word in each gap.

1 We _____ to live in Brazil.
2 Did you _____ to listen to music on CDs?
3 When they were children, they _____ often climb the trees in their garden.
4 I'm not used _____ camping in remote places.
5 She used to _____ a lot of tea, but now she prefers coffee.
6 He never _____ used to living in a flat with no garden.
7 They hated the cold weather at first, but now they _____ used to it.
8 Mark couldn't finish his meal because he wasn't used to _____ so much.
9 How much money did you use _____ get for working in the bookshop?
10 I didn't _____ to like cheese, but I love it now.

Vocabulary

Word formation

8 Complete the sentences with these words.

conclude	discover	explain	remark	reside	ridicule	similar	situate	stick	usual

1 When you _____ something, you find it for the first time.
2 The word _____ means to be or put in a particular place.
3 If you _____ something to something else, you join it with glue.
4 The word _____ means normal.
5 If you _____ somewhere, that's where you live.
6 To _____ means to decide something after studying or thinking about it.
7 Something _____ to another thing is nearly the same as it.
8 When you make a _____ , you say your opinion about something.
9 You _____ something when you make it easy to understand and give information about it.
10 If you _____ something or someone, you make fun of them, and try to make others laugh at them.

9 Use the word in capitals to form a word that fits in the gap.

1 No one understood the teacher's _____ .   EXPLAIN

2 That was a _____ football match.   REMARK

3 It's _____ for it to rain so much in the summer – something strange   USUAL
   is happening to our climate.

4 All the _____ of the tower block had to leave the building when   RESIDE
   the fire alarm went off.

5 That's the most _____ thing I've ever heard!   RIDICULE

6 We found ourselves in a very difficult _____ when we couldn't afford   SITUATE
   to pay our electricity bill.

7 Scientists have made an interesting _____ this month.   DISCOVER

8 What's that _____ stuff on the sofa? Is it chocolate?   STICK

9 I can see the _____ between you and your father.   SIMILAR

10 We finally came to the _____ that it was not a good idea to go   CONCLUDE
   camping that weekend.

Exam practice

Sentence transformation

10 Complete the second sentence so that it has a similar meaning to the first sentence, using the word given. Do not change the word given. You must use between two and five words.

1 On Friday evenings, we usually went to a restaurant in town.
   On Friday evenings, _____ to a restaurant in town.   USED

2 It didn't take long for the girls to adjust to their new life.
   The girls _____ their new life.   GOT

3 Every time we went to the beach, our dog stole someone's ice cream.
   Our dog _____ every time we went to the beach.   WOULD

4 It was difficult for him to drive on the left at first, but now it's easy.
   Now _____ on the left.   IS

5 This club wasn't so popular last year.
   This club _____ so popular last year.   BE

6 Would you check under your bed for monsters when you were a child?
   When you were a child, _____ under your bed for monsters?   TO

7 I never enjoyed going to the theatre, but I do now.
   I _____ going to the theatre, but I do now.   USE

8 Wearing glasses won't bother you after a few days.
   You'll _____ glasses after a few days.   GET

Multiple-choice cloze

11 Read the sentences and decide which answer (A, B, C or D) best fits each gap.

1 I ___ to love riding my skateboard when I was a boy.
  A would   B used   C use   D get

2 It will take a while to ___ used to the busy roads here.
  A get   B have   C be   D do

3 Every day during the summer we ___ take the bus to the seaside.
  A would   B used   C use   D did

4 Did you ___ to enjoy playing in the woods?
  A would   B used   C get   D use

5 He hates it because he ___ not used to it yet.
  A is   B would   C gets   D did

6 How long did it take you to get used to ___ the new computer system?
  A use   B using   C used   D uses

7 We didn't use to ___ much homework in primary school.
  A getting   B got   C get   D gets

8 ___ Sara used to cycling to work every day?
  A Will   B Does   C Has   D Is

Writing

12 Read the writing task and write your answer in 140–190 words in an appropriate style.

You see an announcement in an English-language magazine for young people. They are looking for mystery stories. Write a story beginning with this sentence:

They would often play in the woods near the old castle, but on this particular day, something was different.

Your story must include:

- a mysterious event or place
- a theory or explanation.

Grammar

1 Complete the sentences with the present simple or present continuous form of the verbs.

1 The children _____ (watch) a film about penguins.
2 _____ (you / think) about your exam? Don't worry, I'm sure it'll be fine.
3 How much _____ (the object / weigh)?
4 I _____ (take) guitar lessons this summer.
5 Our train _____ (leave) at 9.35.
6 Mmm – this fish _____ (taste) great!
7 Why _____ (you / be) so silly now?
8 The drawings _____ (not look) like people. I think they're animals.
9 We _____ (not stay) on a campsite.
10 _____ (your dog / enjoy) swimming in the sea?

2 Complete the sentences with *a*, *an*, *the* or – (no article).

1 She always goes to school by _____ bus.
2 I hate Monday mornings – we've got _____ maths from 9 till 11.
3 That's _____ worst joke you've ever told me.
4 Matt goes swimming in the sea for _____ hour every morning.
5 Julia is _____ very good artist.
6 There's _____ entrance to the museum on _____ Highfield Road.
7 We had _____ fantastic holiday in _____ Greece last year.
8 Did you go to _____ exhibition in _____ afternoon?
9 They went to _____ hospital to visit _____ Maria.
10 She has to have _____ operation on _____ New Year's Day.

3 Complete the text with the past simple or past continuous form of the verbs.

I ¹ _____ (work) in my room last night when a message ² _____ (arrive) on my phone. It ³ _____ (be) from an old friend. I ⁴ _____ (read) it, then I ⁵ _____ (go) downstairs to tell my parents about it.

In the living room, my parents ⁶ _____ (watch) TV, and my sister ⁷ _____ (listen) to music on her phone. 'What ⁸ _____ (happen)?' my mum ⁹ _____ (ask) me. 'You look happy.'

'I ¹⁰ _____ (get) an email from Tom,' I ¹¹ _____ (say).

'What ¹² _____ (he / say)?'

I ¹³ _____ (tell) them. 'Tom's coming to visit us this weekend.'

'Oh dear. We ¹⁴ _____ (not expect) any visitors this weekend! I'll have to go shopping,' ¹⁵ _____ (reply) Mum.

When I ¹⁶ _____ (go) back upstairs, my mum ¹⁷ _____ (write) a shopping list. She likes Tom. But my sister ¹⁸ _____ (frown) – she doesn't like any of my friends!

4 Choose the correct option to complete the sentences.

1 This park *used to / would* be much nicer.
2 When I was younger, I *didn't use to / wouldn't* enjoy dancing.
3 She *is / gets* used to working until past midnight.
4 Did it take you long to *be / get* used to living alone?
5 We *were used to / would* watch videos on the internet in the evening.
6 What kind of car *did you use to / would you* drive?
7 Sam soon *was / got* used to his new job.
8 I hated living there because I *didn't get / wasn't* used to such cold weather.

5 Correct the mistakes in these sentences.

1 I'm loving deserts and dry places.

_____

2 These scissors doesn't work.

_____

3 Edinburgh is the capital of the Scotland.

_____

4 They are slowly being used to the new teacher.

_____

5 We were walking in the hills when we were seeing the storm coming.

_____

6 Alex watched never TV.

_____

7 I'd like the new laptop case for my birthday.

_____

8 My parents would to take us on camping holidays.

_____

6 Choose the correct option to complete the sentences.

1 We*'re having / have* a party on Friday.
2 This coffee *is smelling / smells* delicious.
3 Did you enjoy *the / –* food they gave you?
4 I'm going to be *a / the* photographer when I grow up.
5 Simon never *was / got* used to sleeping in a tent.
6 What *did you do / were you doing* when the earthquake happened?
7 I used *to prefer / preferring* caves to mountains.
8 Ella was reading *during / while* the children were playing.

Exam practice

7 For questions 1–8, read the text below and decide which answer (A, B, C or D) best fits each gap. There is an example at the beginning (0).

A spirit of adventure

Adventurers who **(0)** ___ in reaching their goal achieve fame and sometimes fortune. Those who fail have little to **(1)** ___ for their efforts.

A young man from England put aside a large part of his monthly **(2)** ___ for years so that he could cycle down the continent of South America. The **(3)** ___ that he chose meant that he would have to endure extremes, from the freezing cold of the Andes to the humidity of the Amazon jungle.

It was a disaster. He was **(4)** ___ by mosquitoes, he almost drowned while crossing a river which had a much stronger **(5)** ___ than he had imagined, and he was arrested for not having official **(6)** ___ to cross a certain part of Peru. He also had a variety of illnesses and lost so much weight that he couldn't go on. Eventually he was found staggering along a **(7)** ___ mountain path.

Back in Britain, he was interviewed at his **(8)** ___ hospital. When asked about his plans for the future, he answered that he would like to try again!

0	A	manage	B	succeed	C	achieve	D	fulfil
1	A	show	B	exhibit	C	display	D	demonstrate
2	A	investment	B	salary	C	interest	D	money
3	A	way	B	course	C	route	D	track
4	A	stung	B	pecked	C	pinched	D	bitten
5	A	draught	B	drought	C	current	D	flood
6	A	permit	B	permission	C	allowance	D	pass
7	A	remote	B	far	C	distant	D	solitary
8	A	nearby	B	local	C	neighbourhood	D	country

(0 B is circled)

8 For questions 9–16, read the text below and think of the word which best fits each gap. Use only one word in each gap. There is an example at the beginning (0).

Rubber

Malaya is **(0)** ___the___ largest rubber producer in the world. Rubber is produced by making cuts in the bark of a rubber tree, which also cuts the tubes inside that carry a milky liquid containing rubber. The rubber is removed by adding a weak acid to **(9)** ___ milky liquid. A rubber tree can **(10)** ___ tapped for rubber when it is five years **(11)** ___ , and it produces about three kilos of rubber a year.

The name 'rubber' reflects its first technical application. In 1771, it was used to rub out pencil marks **(12)** ___ Joseph Priestly, the British chemist famous for his discovery of oxygen. In 1823, Charles Macintosh, a Scottish chemist **(13)** ___ name has been given to a type of coat, used rubber to make cloth waterproof.

The most widely known process involving rubber is vulcanisation. In 1839, an American, Charles Goodyear, discovered this process, which is **(14)** ___ used today. Vulcanised rubber is quite different **(15)** ___ raw rubber because it becomes five times stronger during vulcanisation, in **(16)** ___ it is heated with sulphur and other ingredients to a temperature of about 150° C.

Grammar

9 For questions 1–10 choose the word or phrase that best completes the sentence.

1 Sara wants to be ___ when she grows up.
A the hairdresser
B a hairdresser
C an hairdresser
D hairdresser

2 'Have you got any plans for the weekend?'
'We ___ to the lake.'
A 're going
B go
C going
D to go

3 'I can't find it anywhere.' 'What ___ ?'
A do you look for
B do you look like
C are you looking for
D are you looking like

4 'Do you know any foreign languages?'
'Yes, I ___ French lessons at school.'
A would take
B was taking
C used to taking
D took

5 'Were you sleeping when I called?' 'Yes, ___ .'
A I was
B I wasn't
C I did
D I slept

6 We always ___ our uncle Matthew.
A would enjoy visiting
B enjoyed to visit
C used to enjoy visiting
D would enjoy to visit

7 I'm afraid we ___ a great time here in Manchester.
A don't have
B aren't having
C not having
D not have

8 What was Susan doing ___ you saw her?
A while
B as
C where
D when

9 I ___ like Tim, but I do now.
A didn't use to
B wasn't used to
C wouldn't
D didn't get used to

10 Did you go on holiday ___ ?
A the last month
B the month ago
C last month
D a last month

Vocabulary

10 For questions 11–20 choose the word or phrase that best completes the sentence.

11 Eva and Ava ___ out again yesterday. They're always arguing!
A got
B kept
C hung
D fell

12 I got so angry – I saw ___ !
A pink
B blue
C red
D green

13 Max and Mo have the same sense ___ humour.
A of
B on
C in
D for

14 'What does that sign say?'
'I'm not sure. I can't ___ it out in this light.'
A do
B see
C take
D make

15 I don't believe him. I think he's ___ it up.
A taking
B making
C looking
D giving

16 Do you ___ in touch with your old friends?
A fall
B hang
C have
D keep

17 I don't ___ of phones at the dinner table.
A agree
B approve
C accept
D admit

18 I don't have a lot in ___ with my brother.
A nerves
B touch
C common
D natural

19 They're ___ into some possible causes.
A looking
B finding
C working
D being

20 Are you feeling nervous ___ flying?
A in
B across
C about
D with

1 Which of these sentences are correct (C) and incorrect (I)?

1 She has worked here for seven years. ___
2 You've won a fantastic prize just. ___
3 George has been ride his bike all afternoon. ___
4 Have you been crying? ___
5 Dan has been breaking his finger. ___
6 Where have they been hiding? ___
7 I've lived here since two months. ___
8 You haven't been concentrating. ___
9 We've been here twice so far. ___
10 He hasn't seen his grandmother for April. ___

How many did you get right? ☐

Grammar

Present perfect simple

Affirmative	Negative	Questions
I / We / You / They **have** (**'ve**) start**ed**. He / She / It **has** (**'s**) start**ed**.	I / We / You / They **have not** (**haven't**) start**ed**. He / She / It **has not** (**hasn't**) start**ed**.	**Have** I / we / you / they start**ed**? **Has** he / she / it start**ed**?
Short Answers		
Yes, I / we / you / they **have**. **Yes**, he / she / it **has**.	**No**, I / we / you / they **haven't**. **No**, he / she / it **hasn't**.	

Spelling: work → work**ed**, dance → danc**ed**, travel → travel**led**, study → stu**died**, play → pla**yed**

We use the present perfect simple for:

- something that started in the past and has continued until now.
*We **have lived** in this flat for three years.*

- something that happened in the past, but we don't know or we don't say exactly when.
*She **has qualified** as a yoga instructor.*

- something that happened in the past and has a result that affects the present.
*He **has injured** his leg, so he can't climb the mountain.*

- actions that have just finished.
*I**'ve just heard** the news.*

- experiences and achievements.
*My sister **has run** the London Marathon three times.*

> **Note**
>
> Some verbs are irregular and do not follow these spelling rules. See a list of irregular verbs and their past participles on pages 145–146.

> **Note**
>
> Some common time expressions that are often used with the present perfect simple are *already, ever, for, for a long time / ages, just, never, once, recently, since 2019 / March, so far, twice, three times, until now, yet,* etc.
> *I've been to the gym **three times** this week.*

> **Remember**
>
> We use *have / has been* when someone has gone somewhere and has now returned, but we use *have / has gone* when someone has gone somewhere and is still there.
> *Simon **has been** to New Zealand. He showed us his photos last night.*
> *Simon **has gone** to New Zealand. He will be back next week.*

Present perfect continuous

Affirmative	Negative	Questions
I / We / You / They **have** (**'ve**) **been talking**. He / She / It **has** (**'s**) **been** talk**ing**.	I / We / You / They **have not** (**haven't**) **been** talk**ing**. He / She / it **has not** (**hasn't**) **been** talk**ing**.	**Have** I / we / you / they **been** talk**ing**? **Has** he / she / it **been** talk**ing**?
Short Answers		
Yes, I / we / you / they **have**. **Yes**, he / she / it **has**.	**No**, I / we / you / they **haven't**. **No**, he / she / it **hasn't**.	

Spelling: take → tak**ing**, run → runn**ing**, study → stu**dying**

We use the present perfect continuous:

- for actions that started in the past and are still in progress now or have happened repeatedly until now.
*We **have been growing** our own vegetables for years.*

- for actions that happened repeatedly in the past and have finished recently, but that have results that affect the present.
*The dog is wet because it**'s been swimming** in the river.*

- to emphasise how long actions have been in progress for.
*It's **been raining** for six weeks!*

> **Note**
>
> Some common time expressions that are often used with the present perfect continuous are *all day / night / week, for years / a long time / ages, lately, recently, since*. We can use *How long ...?* with the present perfect continuous in questions and *for (very) long* in questions and negative sentences.
> ***How long** have you been learning Japanese?*
> *She's been working on this project **for months**.*
> *I haven't been training **for long**.*

Present perfect simple and continuous

We use the present perfect simple to talk about something we have done or achieved, or an action that is complete. It is also used to say how many times something happened.
*We have visited our cousins in Canada **twice**.*

We use the present perfect continuous to talk about how long something has been happening. It is not important whether or not it has finished.
*Nadia has been swimming **for ages**.*

for, since, lately, already, yet and still

We use *for* with an expression that shows a period of time at the end of a sentence with the present perfect simple.
*My mum hasn't eaten meat **for** twenty years.*

We use *since* with a point of time in the past at the end of a sentence with the present perfect simple.
*She's been vegetarian **since** 2001.*

We use *lately* with the present perfect to mean *at a time in the recent past or not long ago*. It normally goes at the end of the question or statement.
*Has she been going to the gym **lately**?*
*He has been doing more exercise **lately**.*

We use *already* with the present perfect simple to mean *at some point before now*. Already can go between the auxiliary verb and the past participle or at the end of the sentence.
*I have **already** replied to your email. / I have replied to your email **already**.*
*Have you **already** had lunch? / Have you had lunch **already**?*

We use *yet* with the present perfect simple in negative statements and questions to talk about things that have not happened before now. It usually goes at the end of the sentence.
*I haven't been to the new swimming pool **yet**.*
*Have you entered the fun run **yet**?*

We use *still* with the present perfect in a negative sentence to show that something hasn't happened, but that we expect it to.
*They **still** haven't found a cure for the common cold.*

5

Grammar exercises

2 **Choose the correct option to complete the sentences.**

1 *Have you heard / Have you been hearing* the weather forecast?
2 The doctor *has given / has been giving* me a new prescription.
3 There you are! *Have you avoided / Have you been avoiding* me deliberately?
4 Rachel *has swum / has been swimming* – that's why her hair is wet.
5 Oh no! *We have missed / have been missing* the start of the game.
6 How long *have you tried / have you been trying* to phone me?
7 I *haven't seen / haven't been seeing* Julia for weeks.
8 We're tired because we *'ve done / 've been doing* aerobics.
9 He *'s visited / 's been visiting* the dentist twice this month.
10 Sorry I'm late. *Have you waited / Have you been waiting* for ages?

3 **Complete the sentences with *been* or *gone*.**

1 Tina isn't here. She's _____ shopping. She'll be back soon.
2 I've _____ shopping. Look what I bought!
3 We'd love to go to Australia. We've never _____ there.
4 The children aren't here. They've _____ to their grandparents' house.
5 Have you ever _____ to a hockey match?
6 Dad has _____ on a bike ride. I don't know when he'll be home.
7 Has Jack _____ to school already? He's left his bag on the table!
8 I don't have your medication because I haven't _____ to the pharmacy yet.

4 **Complete the conversation with the present perfect simple or present perfect continuous form of the verbs.**

Alex: Oh, there you are, Oscar. I ¹ _____ (look) for you all morning. Where
² _____ (you / be)?

Oscar: I ³ _____ (help) Sophie fix her bike. It's really old. She ⁴ _____ (have) it for about five years now.

Alex: I know. I wonder why she ⁵ _____ (not ask) her parents to buy her a new one?

Oscar: Her dad's business ⁶ _____ (not do) well for years, so they haven't got much money. Anyway – why ⁷ _____ (you / look) for me? What ⁸ _____ (happen)?

Sophie: The back wheel ⁹ _____ (come) off my skateboard, and I don't know how to put it on again. Can you help?

Oscar: Of course. I ¹⁰ _____ (fix) skateboards for years. I'm sure it won't be a problem!

5 **Choose the correct option (a–c) to complete the sentences.**

1 Harry has been feeling ill ___ dinner time.
  a for   **b** since   **c** still

2 I ___ haven't heard from my new pen pal.
  a yet   **b** lately   **c** still

3 They haven't done their homework ___.
  a yet   **b** for   **c** still

4 Have you been losing weight ___ ?
  a still   **b** lately   **c** for

5 She's been in hospital ___ nearly two weeks.
  a for   **b** lately   **c** yet

6 Have you finished ___ ? That was quick!
  a already   **b** yet   **c** lately

6 Complete the questions.

1 A: ___*What medication have you been taking*___ ?
   B: I haven't been taking any medication.
2 A: How long _____ ?
   B: I've been going to yoga classes for three months.
3 A: Where _____ my vitamins?
   B: I haven't put them anywhere! You had them in your hand a minute ago.
4 A: What _____ to your arm?
   B: I broke it when I was playing rugby.
5 A: Why _____ ?
   B: I've been avoiding fatty foods because I'm trying to eat more healthily.
6 A: _____ on the beach today?
   B: Yes, the kids have been playing on the beach all morning. Are their feet sandy?

7 Correct the sentences where necessary. Tick (✓) those which do not need correcting.

1 We've been growing our own food since years.

2 This restaurant has been serving vegetarian food since 1980.

3 How many times have I been telling you not to eat so much meat?

4 Have you seen the doctor about your problem still?

5 Has he already left for the gym?

6 I haven't had any healthy food for last weekend.

Vocabulary

Prepositions

8 Complete the phrases with these prepositions. Some prepositions can be used more than once.

against   of   on   over   to

1 at risk _____
2 a member _____
3 be _____ (100 years old)
4 contribute _____

5 depend _____
6 focus _____
7 protect _____
8 work _____

9 Complete the sentences with the phrases from Exercise 8.

1 Some cats can live to _____ 15 years old.
2 I can't come out because I need to _____ my geography project.
3 Mark doesn't know which university he is going to – it _____ his exam results.
4 When you concentrate on one thing, you _____ it.
5 If you don't wear a helmet when riding, you are _____ serious injury.

6 People sometimes use their cars unnecessarily, which _____ pollution in this city.

7 How long have you been _____ this tennis club?

8 Children may suffer if they are not _____ diseases in early life.

Exam practice

10 **Complete the second sentence so that it has a similar meaning to the first sentence, using the word given. Do not change the word given. You must use between two and five words.**

1 Mum is still cooking this evening's meal.

   Mum _____ this evening's meal yet.   **NOT**

2 I started French lessons two years ago.

   I _____ two years.   **LEARNING**

3 Swimming all afternoon has made me feel very hungry.

   I feel very hungry because _____ all afternoon.   **BEEN**

4 She met Jake six months ago.

   She _____ six months.   **KNOWN**

5 The Smiths are on holiday in Greece.

   The Smiths _____ on holiday.   **TO**

6 It's a long time since we have been to London.

   We haven't _____ a long time.   **FOR**

7 He moved there in 2018 and he still lives there.

   He _____ 2018.   **LIVING**

8 It started raining four days ago, and it hasn't stopped yet.

   It _____ four days.   **FOR**

Word formation

11 **Use the word in capitals to form a word that fits in the gap.**

1 My cousin is training to be a fitness _____ .   **INSTRUCT**

2 I went to the doctor and he _____ my leg.   **EXAM**

3 Try to reduce your _____ of carbohydrates, and you might lose weight.   **CONSUME**

4 Maria suffers from a rare _____ disease which means she has to take medicine every day.   **GENE**

5 Do you feel you are under a lot of _____ to succeed at work?   **PRESS**

6 Simon is so healthy – he has never had a serious _____ in his life.   **ILL**

7 I'm sorry – I _____ restarted your computer, and now you have lost your work.   **ACCIDENT**

8 We like to go out and _____ with friends every Friday night.   **SOCIAL**

Writing

12 **Write five sentences in your notebook saying what you, your family, and your friends have NEVER done. Then write five more sentences saying what you have been doing, and for how long.**

Unit 6

Awareness

1 Which of these sentences are correct (C) and incorrect (I)?

1 Welcome to the show, ladys and gentlemen. ___
2 There are some tomatoes in the fridge. ___
3 You have very white tooths. ___
4 Our research show that fruit is very healthy. ___
5 May I have a loaf of cheese, please? ___

6 Fresh food is good for you. ___
7 The news were very upsetting. ___
8 I'm sorry, your luggage is too heavy. ___
9 How much friends do you have? ___
10 There's a few milk left in the bottle. ___

How many did you get right? ☐

Grammar

Countable nouns

Most nouns are countable and have singular and plural forms.
Some are regular and add -s or -es and others are irregular.

mountain → mountains	toy → toys	leaf → leaves	man → men
potato → potatoes	baby → babies	fish → fish	foot → feet

We usually use *a* or *an* with singular countable nouns.
a doctor   *an instructor*

We can use *some*, *any* or a number (e.g. *three*) with plural countable nouns.
*I've prepared **some** vegetables.*
*Are there **any** apples in the fruit bowl?*
*She's been doing yoga for **five** months.*

We use singular or plural verb forms with countable nouns depending on whether we are talking about one or more things.
*An orange **contains** a lot of vitamin C.*
*Oranges **are** good for you.*

Remember

Some countable nouns don't end in -s . Remember to use a plural verb form with them.
*The children **are** in the garden.*
*The dentist said her teeth **were** very healthy.*

Uncountable nouns

Some nouns are uncountable. They do not have plural forms.

advice	fun	luggage	rubbish
biology	furniture	medicine	salt
cheese	health	milk	time
chocolate	history	money	traffic
equipment	homework	music	water
food	information	progress	weather
fruit	knowledge	research	

We don't use *a* or *an* with uncountable nouns. We can use *some* and *any*.
*We need to buy **some** bread.*
*Have you got **any** money?*

We always use singular verb forms with uncountable nouns.
*That **music is** amazing. What is it?*
*The **information isn't** available yet.*

6

Some uncountable nouns end in -s. Remember to use a singular verb form with them.

*Is the **athletics** on TV this afternoon?*
***Physics is** my least favourite subject.*

We can use phrases describing quantity with uncountable nouns to say how much we have. These are the most common phrases.

a *bag of*	a *jar of*
a *bottle of*	a *kilo of*
a *bowl of*	a *loaf of*
a *can / tin of*	a *number of*
a *carton of*	a *packet of*
a *cup / glass of*	a *piece of*

*I'd like **a glass of** water.*
*There's **a bag of** crisps on the table.*

Quantifiers

We use *some* with both uncountable and plural countable nouns in affirmative sentences and in requests or offers.
*We've made **some pancakes**.*
*Could I **have some** milk, please?*
*Would you like **some help** with the cooking?*

We use *any* with both uncountable and plural countable nouns in negative sentences and in questions.
*Kate doesn't want **any coffee**.*
*Have you got **any brothers**?*

We use *a lot / lots of* with both uncountable and plural countable nouns.
*Do you do **a lot / lots of exercise** every week?*
*There's **a lot / lots of fruit** in the bowl.*

We use *a little* with uncountable nouns and *a few* with plural countable nouns in affirmative sentences.
*There's **a little juice** left, if you want some.*
*There were **a few people** playing tennis in the rain.*

We use *much* with uncountable nouns and *many* with plural countable nouns in negative sentences and in questions.
*How **much homework** do we have this week?*
*There aren't **many gyms** which allow children.*

Grammar exercises

2 **Complete the sentences with the plurals of the nouns.**

1 Modern medicine has saved a lot of _____ . (life)

2 The life expectancy for _____ in Okinawa is 78 years. (man)

3 Dentists recommend that you brush your _____ after every meal or snack. (tooth)

4 It is important for _____ to get plenty of exercise. (child)

5 _____ can begin eating solid food at around six months of age. (baby)

6 We made a healthy salad with onions, peppers and some lettuce _____ . (leaf)

7 How many _____ are in your singing group? (person)

8 Did you catch many _____ yesterday? (fish)

9 I drink five large _____ of water every day. (glass)

10 Can you buy some _____ , please? (tomato)

3 Complete the table with these nouns.

accident   brain   calorie   energy   evidence   health
injury   milk   pain   operation   soap   symptom

| COUNTABLE | _____ _____ | _____ _____ | _____ _____ |
| UNCOUNTABLE | _____ _____ | _____ _____ | _____ _____ |

4 Complete the sentences with *a*, *an*, *some* or *any*.

1 We need to buy _____ bandages.
2 Does _____ apple a day really keep the doctor away?
3 I'm sorry, I don't have _____ medicine to give you.
4 You need _____ of my homemade chicken soup.
5 Have you got _____ pills for a headache?
6 There's _____ bowl of fruit in the kitchen – help yourself!
7 I need to make _____ appointment with my doctor.
8 That's _____ painful looking injury!

5 Choose the correct option to complete the sentences.

1 Don't forget to take a *bottle / bag* of water to the gym with you.
2 Can I have a *loaf / piece* of cheese, please?
3 Every morning, I drink two *jars / cups* of tea.
4 We need a *loaf / packet* of bread.
5 How do you get through a whole *jar / glass* of honey every week?
6 Would you like a *can / piece* of lemonade?

6 Choose the correct option (a–c) to complete the sentences.

1 I'm afraid we don't eat ___ of healthy food in our family.
   a much   b a lot   c many

2 Dan has ___ questions to ask the doctor.
   a a few   b a little   c a lot

3 Very ___ people take enough exercise.
   a much   b little   c few

4 Please may I have ___ money to buy a snack at break time?
   a a little   b a lot   c a few

5 There's ___ point in going on a diet if you don't do any exercise.
   a much   b few   c little

6 We don't have ___ time to do this project.
   a many   b a lot   c much

7 There are ___ things you can do to improve your health and fitness.
   a many   b a lot   c much

8 Always drink ___ of water when the weather is hot.
   a many   b a few   c lots

7 Write questions with *How much* or *How many*.

1 _____

I've been to the gym three times this week.

2 _____

There's about a litre of water in the bottle.

3 _____

I've spent five pounds today.

4 _____

I've been sitting here for two hours.

5 _____

I need two cups of rice.

6 _____

He's had a lot of experience.

7 _____

I've been in hospital once.

8 _____

She drinks a lot of coffee every day – sometimes five cups.

Vocabulary

Collocations and expressions

8 Match the expressions (1–8) with their meanings (a–h).

1	do you the world of good	☐	a	regain energy
2	fit as a fiddle	☐	b	extremely exhausted
3	lease of life	☐	c	starting to feel better
4	on my last legs	☐	d	feel slightly unwell
5	on the mend	☐	e	a chance of better health
6	pick someone's brains	☐	f	very fit and well
7	recharge your batteries	☐	g	make you feel much better
8	under the weather	☐	h	ask an expert for information or advice

9 Complete the sentences with the phrases from Exercise 8.

1 Anu, can I _____ ? I don't know anything about computers.

2 That long holiday has given them a new _____ .

3 My great-grandmother is 94, but she's as _____ .

4 I really need a holiday to _____ after doing all those exams.

5 Jack has been running non-stop for nearly six hours, and now he's _____ .

6 Drink this. It will _____ .

7 I'm not really ill – I'm just feeling a bit _____ , that's all.

8 Three months after he broke his arm, Adam is finally _____ and hopes to play tennis next week.

Exam practice

Sentence transformation

10 Complete the second sentence so that it has a similar meaning to the first sentence, using the word given. Do not change the word given. You must use between two and five words

1 You don't need to spend a lot of money to have a healthy diet.
You only need _____ to have a healthy diet.   **LITTLE**

2 I didn't go out because I wasn't feeling very well.
I was _____ , so I didn't go out.   **WEATHER**

3 There are very few gyms in this town.
There _____ gyms in this town.   **MANY**

4 You'll feel much better after a good night's sleep.
A good night's sleep will _____ good.   **WORLD**

5 Three or four ideas mentioned at the meeting were really interesting.
There were _____ mentioned at the meeting.   **FEW**

6 We have very little food left in the house.
We _____ food left in the house.   **MUCH**

7 He had to work really hard to get picked for the team.
He had to do _____ to get picked for the team.   **LOT**

8 By the time she got home, she was absolutely exhausted.
She was _____ by the time she got home.   **LEGS**

Open cloze

11 Read the sentences and think of a word which best fits each gap. Use only one word in each gap.

1 We haven't got _____ money in the bank.

2 You certainly eat a lot _____ vegetables, don't you?

3 I'm afraid the news _____ not good.

4 Can you get _____ carton of pineapple juice from the shop, please?

5 I take just a _____ sugar in my tea, thank you.

6 Harry has _____ allergy to cats.

7 How _____ times a week do you go swimming?

8 There's a little medicine left in the bottle, but not _____ .

Writing

12 Read the writing task and write your answer in 140–190 words in an appropriate style.

You see an advert on an English-speaking website asking for articles. Write an article answering these questions:

What is the secret to a long and happy life?
What advice would you give in terms of food, exercise and health?
What is the most useful thing you have ever learned?

Unit 7

Awareness

1 Which of these sentences are correct (C) and incorrect (I)?

1 I'll text you when I leave. ___
2 Sam is going make a pizza tonight. ___
3 Our flight leave at 07.45. ___
4 When we finish this game, we'll stop. ___
5 I let you know as soon as I arrive. ___

6 He's going to winning this race! ___
7 Donna will meeting you tomorrow. ___
8 I'm not going to help you with this. ___
9 Don't do anything until I'll get there. ___
10 After you've revised, you'll feel better. ___

How many did you get right? ☐

Grammar

will

Affirmative	Negative	Questions
I / He / She / It / We / You / They **will** work.	I / He / She / It / We / You / They **will not (won't)** work.	**Will** I / he / she / it / we / you / they **work**?
Short Answers		
Yes, I / he / she / it / we / you / they **will.**	**No,** I / he / she / it / we / you / they **won't.**	

We use *will*:
- for decisions made at the time of speaking.
I'll download the software tonight.
- for predictions.
*Most people born now **will live** to be over 100 years old.*
- for promises and offers of help.
*I promise **I'll buy** you a new tablet.*
***I'll pick you up** at the station if you like.*
- for threats.
*Stop using your phone or **I'll tell** the teacher.*
- to talk about future facts.
*The new museum **will open** on April 10th.*
- after verbs like *think, believe, be sure, expect,* etc. and words like *probably, maybe,* etc.
*I think they**'ll deliver** the keyboards tomorrow.*
- to ask someone to do something.
***Will you lock** the door when you leave, please?*

> **Note**
>
> We use *shall* with *I* and *we* in questions or when we want to make a suggestion or an offer.
> ***What** websites **shall we** use for our research?*
> ***Shall we** go to the technology fair?*
> ***Shall I** show you how the app works?*

be going to

Affirmative	Negative	Questions
I am **('m) going to** work. He /She / It **is ('s) going to** work. We / You / They **are ('re) going to** work.	I am **('m) not going to** work. He / She / It **is not (isn't) going to** work. We / You / They **are not (aren't) going to** work.	**Am** I **going to** work? **Is** he / she / it **going to** work? **Are** we / you / they **going to** work?
Yes, I am. Yes, we / you / they **are.** Yes, he / she / it **is.**	**No,** I'm not. **No,** we / you / they **aren't.** **No,** he / she / it **isn't.**	

We use *be going to* for:

- future plans.

I'm going to buy *a new printer at the weekend.*

- predictions for the near future based on present situations or evidence.

My phone battery is only on 7%. ***I'm going to need*** *a charger cable.*

> **Note**
>
> Some common time expressions that are often used with *will* and *be going to* are *this week / month / summer, tonight, this evening, tomorrow, tomorrow morning / afternoon / night, next week / month / year, at the weekend, in February, in a few minutes / hours / days, on Friday, on Monday morning,* etc.
> *It's OK, I'll check the database* **tomorrow morning**.
> *We're going to start the video call* **in a few minutes**.

Time expressions

When we use time expressions such as *when, before, after, until, by the time, the moment,* etc. to talk about the future, we use them with a present tense. We do not use them with a future tense.
After I finish *my homework, you can use my tablet.*
The exhibition will be closed ***by the time*** *we* ***get*** *there.*

We use the present perfect simple to emphasise that the first action is finished before the other one starts.
You can play computer games ***when*** *you****'ve eaten*** *your dinner.* (You'll eat first and then you'll play.)
As soon as *everyone* ***has eaten****, we'll start the game.* (Everyone will eat first and then we'll start.)

Grammar exercises

2 **Choose the correct option to complete the sentences.**

1 We'll go to the new museum *when / until* it opens.

2 *Will / Shall* I help you with that?

3 *By the time / The moment* we have the answer, we'll call you.

4 *After / Before* you've finished your exams, we'll celebrate.

5 In 100 years' time, humans *will live / are going to live* on Mars.

6 Watch out! That fence *will fall / is going to fall*.

7 *Will / Shall* you do the washing-up, please?

8 I'm sure they*'ll / 're going to* understand.

3 **Complete the conversation with *will* or *going to* and the verbs.**

Sam: Hi, Julia. Do you want to come to the town centre with me?

Julia: Have you seen the weather forecast? It [1] _____ (rain).

Sam: That's OK – I [2] _____ (bring) an umbrella. Come on! I think Dan and Sara [3] _____ (be) there.

Julia: I don't care. I [4] _____ (stay) in today.

Sam: Oh, come on, Julia. I [5] _____ (pick) you up on my scooter.

Julia: No. I [6] _____ (sit) on the sofa with my laptop and play games all afternoon.

Sam: What game [7] _____ (you / play)?

Julia: I [8] _____ (try) out the new football game my dad gave me.

Sam: Oh, [9] I'm sure that _____ (be) lots of fun!

Julia: Do you want to come round?

Sam: I [10] _____ (get) my coat!

4 Complete the sentences with these verbs using *will* or the present simple form.

> arrive   buy   give   leave   open   see   send   speak

1 Let's wait here until the café _____ .
2 I _____ you my phone number before I go.
3 What are you going to do when you _____ school?
4 We _____ him an email as soon as we know his exam results.
5 You should tidy up before your parents _____ home.
6 Once we've moved to our new house, we _____ some new furniture.
7 The doctor _____ you as soon as she's ready.
8 Give Tanya this note when you _____ to her, please.

5 Complete the sentences with the verbs using *will* or the present simple form.

1 We like to play tennis when the weather _____ (be) nice.
2 Let's go home before it _____ (start) raining.
3 I _____ (tell) you all about my day when I get back.
4 Judy _____ (write) her report as soon as she has gathered all the information.
5 When I get my new phone, I _____ (be) able to take some great photos.
6 We _____ (wait) until you have WiFi before we _____ (come) and visit you.
7 _____ (you / have) a shower before you _____ (go) out tonight?
8 I _____ (ask) him the next time I _____ (see) him.

6 Choose the correct option (a–c) to complete the sentences.

1 Don't go out until the rain ___ .
   a stopped   b will stop   c stops

2 Will you visit us ___ you are in the country?
   a when   b before   c until

3 I ___ you my new camera when I see you.
   a show   b 'll show   c 've shown

4 Do you want a drink before you ___ to bed?
   a go   b 'll go   c 've gone

5 You're not leaving ___ you answer my question.
   a when   b until   c after

6 I'll have a bath ___ I get home.
   a the moment   b until   c before

7 She ___ sad when she finally leaves school.
   a 's   b 'll be   c 's been

8 I ___ my homework as soon as I can.
   a finished   b 'll finished   c 'll finish

7 Complete the sentences.

1 You'll pass all your exams. We'll have a party then.
We _____*'ll have a party*_____ when _____*you pass all your exams*_____ .

2 I'll get a new phone. I'll give you my number.
I _____ as soon as _____ .

3 My mum must give me permission first. I won't go out until then.
_____ until _____ .

4 You'll arrive this evening. But the children will already be in bed.
When _____ .

5 The technician must fix the computers. Then we'll start work.
_____ when _____ .

6 A thunder storm is going to start. Let's go back to the car before it does.
_____ before _____ .

7 I'll buy some food. Then I'll come home and cook.
_____ as soon as _____ .

8 This film will end. Then we will go for a meal.
_____ after _____ .

Vocabulary

Word formation

8 Match the words (1–8) with their meanings (a–h).

1	attract	☐	a	make something happen or exist
2	compete	☐	b	make someone want to do something
3	connect	☐	c	arrange or plan something
4	create	☐	d	burst with force
5	explode	☐	e	take part in a game and try to win
6	inspire	☐	f	design or produce something new
7	invent	☐	g	make someone / something interested
8	organise	☐	h	join two or more things together

9 Use the word in capitals to form a word that fits in the gap.

1 Are you sure your phone is _____ to the WiFi?   CONNECT
2 I think the blue and green laptop case is the most _____ .   ATTRACT
3 Kate's desk is very well _____ . There's a place for everything.   ORGANISE
4 The teacher gave an _____ talk to the new students.   INSPIRE
5 The firework display turned the night sky into an _____ of colour .   EXPLODE
6 What do you think has been the most important _____ in human history?   INVENT
7 Congratulations on winning a prize in the science _____ .   COMPETE
8 There were some really _____ suggestions in the meeting.   CREATE

7

Exam practice

10 Complete the second sentence so that it has a similar meaning to the first sentence, using the word given. Do not change the word given. You must use between two and five words.

1 I've decided not to do this homework until tomorrow morning.

I _____ this homework until tomorrow morning. **GOING**

2 I expect Maria will pass all her exams.

I _____ fail any of her exams. **SURE**

3 Computer science is what he intends to study at university.

He _____ computer science at university. **GOING**

4 I'll only help you if you apologise to Rachel.

I won't _____ you apologise to Rachel. **UNTIL**

5 She's saving her money to buy a laptop.

She'll _____ she has saved enough money. **WHEN**

6 When you get to school, go and see the head teacher immediately.

Go and see the head teacher _____ to school. **SOON**

7 When I left the house it started to rain.

It started to rain _____ the house. **MOMENT**

8 When we get there, the party will be over.

The party will be over _____ get there. **TIME**

Open cloze

11 Read the sentences and think of a word which best fits each gap. Use only one word in each gap.

1 Your phone's ringing. I _____ answer it.

2 What are you going _____ buy Tim for his birthday?

3 _____ they going to the conference with you?

4 Will _____ be a scanner in my new office?

5 They should be ready _____ the time we get there.

6 I think I'll fall asleep _____ moment my head touches the pillow.

7 Tell him to wait there _____ I've spoken to his teacher.

8 As _____ as the sun comes out, we'll go to the park.

Writing

12 Write a paragraph in your notebook.
How do you think the world will be different in 15 years' time?

1 Which of these sentences are correct (C) and incorrect (I)?

1 You won't finished by 5 p.m. ___

2 The food will have gone before we arrive. ___

3 She'll have left by the time you got home. ___

4 You can go to the park when you'll do the dishes. ___

5 We'll have lived here for eight years next month. ___

6 This time next year you'll be studying art. ___

7 He's getting a new computer when he'll save enough money. ___

8 This time tomorrow we'll be flown to Japan. ___

9 I'll help you after this game will be over. ___

10 We'll be lying on the beach this time next week. ___

How many did you get right? ☐

Grammar

Future continuous

Affirmative	Negative	Questions
I / He / She / It / We / You / They **will be working**.	I / He / She / It / We / You / They **will not (won't) be** working.	**Will** I / he / she /it / we / you / they **be** working?
Short Answers		
Yes, I / he / she / it / we / you / they **will**.	**No**, I / he / she / it / we / you / they **won't**.	

Spelling: save → sa**ving**, travel → trave**lling**, study → stu**dying**

We use the future continuous for:

• actions that will be in progress at a specific time in the future.
We'll be learning about cloning this afternoon.

• plans and arrangements for the future.
Nick will be joining us for the design meeting.

> **Note**
>
> Some common time expressions that are often used with the future continuous are *this time next week / month / summer, this time tomorrow morning / afternoon / night,* etc. **This time next month**, we**'ll be using** the new IT system.

Future perfect simple

Affirmative	Negative	Questions
I / he / she / it / we / you / they **will have** work**ed**.	I / he / she / it / we / you / they **will not (won't) have** work**ed**.	**Will** I / he / she / it / we / you / they **have** work**ed**?
Short Answers		
Yes, I / he / she / it / we / you / they **will**.	**No**, I / he / she / it / we / you / they **won't**.	

Spelling: start → start**ed**, save → sav**ed**, travel → trave**lled**, study → stu**died**, play → play**ed**

We use the future perfect simple to talk about:

• something that will be finished by or before a specific time in the future.
I'll have finished creating this website by Wednesday.

• the length of time that an action will have lasted for at a point of time in the future.
They'll have lived here for a year at the end of this month.

> **Note**
>
> Some verbs are irregular and do not follow these spelling rules. See a list of irregular verbs and their past participles on pages 145–146.

8

Grammar exercises

2 **Choose the correct option to complete the sentences.**

1 In 2050, robots *will have controlled / will be controlling* the whole world.
2 Don't phone me after dinner because I *will watch / will be watching* TV.
3 By this time tomorrow, they *are finishing / will have finished* updating the website.
4 I have to get up early tomorrow, so I *leave / am leaving* in a minute.
5 They *will be sleeping / are sleeping* by the time you arrive.
6 By the end of next month, we'll *have worked / be working* on this project for a year.
7 Hurry up! The bus *will have left / leaves* in less than five minutes!
8 This time next year, I *will be working / am working* as a software designer.

3 **Complete the sentences with *will* or the future continuous form of the verbs.**

1 I _____ (lend) you my laptop, if you like.
2 We _____ (sit) on a plane this time tomorrow.
3 I expect Greg _____ (be) home by now.
4 _____ (you / turn on) the light, please?
5 Come and visit when you want. I _____ (not do) anything important.
6 I think everyone in the world _____ (have) a smartphone by 2040.
7 Don't call him between 7.30 and 8.00 because he _____ (watch) his favourite show.
8 _____ (you / eat) dinner in the restaurant this evening, madam?

4 **Complete the sentences with the future perfect simple or future continuous form of the verbs.**

1 By December, I _____ (have) this same laptop for six years.
2 In the year 2100, all human beings _____ (live) under water.
3 When I'm sixty, I still _____ (not learn) everything about robotics.
4 This time next year, I _____ (study) physics at university.
5 The head teacher's plan is that tablets _____ (replace) books in all classes by the end of next year.
6 At the end of this term, Mrs Jones _____ (work) through the whole course book with us.
7 Please don't phone me tonight – I _____ (do) my homework until bedtime.
8 We aren't late. The match _____ (not start) yet.

5 Choose the correct option (a–c) to complete the sentences.

1 From next year, we ___ in a house nearer my school.
   a will live   b will be living   c will have lived

2 ___ cooking by seven o'clock?
   a Shall you finish   b Will you be finishing   c Will you have finished

3 Do you think Mrs Scott ___ to the head teacher yet?
   a will speak   b will be speaking   c will have spoken

4 How long ___ each other by the end of this year?
   a will we have known   b will we be knowing   c will we know

5 Be quiet when you get home tonight. We ___ .
   a are going to sleep   b will be sleeping   c will have slept

6 What time ___ their presentation?
   a shall they give   b will they be giving   c will they have given

6 Complete the sentences with one word in each gap.

1 Will you _____ completed this by five o'clock?

2 The next flight to Madrid departs _____ 5.15.

3 I think we'll still be _____ lunch at that time.

4 She _____ going for a run later this morning.

5 In five years' time, the computer you are using will _____ become useless.

6 Every student will _____ using this technology in the classroom by this time next year.

7 Correct the mistakes in these sentences.

1 I'll giving a talk on internet security next weekend.

   _____

2 By the end of the year, I'll be completing my course.

   _____

3 Tom won't be finished the project yet.

   _____

4 Shall you help me, please?

   _____

5 I'm not going cook this evening.

   _____

6 Simon won't have come with us tomorrow.

   _____

7 This time next week, I'll relax.

   _____

8 Shall I be showing you how to use this software?

   _____

8

Vocabulary

Phrasal verbs

8 Match the phrasal verbs (1–8) with their meanings (a–h).

1 back up	☐	**a**	stop a machine or computer from working
2 back out	☐	**b**	connect to an electricity supply or another piece of equipment
3 come up with	☐	**c**	turn on a machine or light by pressing a button
4 log in	☐	**d**	save a copy of your work
5 plug in	☐	**e**	prepare or organise
6 set up	☐	**f**	think of and create something new
7 shut down	☐	**g**	decide not to do something you had arranged to do
8 switch on	☐	**h**	gain access to a computer

9 Complete the sentences with the correct form of the phrasal verbs from Exercise 8.

1 Please _____ your devices when you've finished using them.

2 Can you _____ a meeting for next Tuesday afternoon?

3 Oh no! I forgot to _____ the washing machine, so my clothes are still dirty.

4 The monitor didn't work because it wasn't _____ to the computer.

5 We didn't know what to do until Sam _____ a brilliant idea.

6 Always _____ your work! You'll lose it if you don't.

7 I'm sorry, I'm going to have to _____ of this project – I've got too much work to do.

8 The network is down, so I can't _____ to my account at the moment.

Exam practice

Sentence transformation

10 Complete the second sentence so that it has a similar meaning to the first sentence, using the word given. Do not change the word given. You must use between two and five words.

1 You can phone me before 11 p.m. because I will be awake.

I _____ before 11 p.m., so you can phone me.　　**SLEEPING**

2 Sam will be there by now, I expect.

I expect Sam _____ by now.　　**ARRIVED**

3 What time is the match tomorrow?

What time _____ tomorrow?　　**START**

4 My room will be redecorated by Sunday.

We _____ my room by Sunday.　　**HAVE**

5 Five o'clock is when we leave.

We _____ five o'clock.　　**ARE**

6 I'll log off after I've saved my work.

I'll _____ before I log off.　　**BACK**

7 We're going to stay here until we can find a solution.

We're not leaving until _____ a solution.　　**COME**

8 Is there a place where I can connect my charger cable to a power supply?

Is there a place where _____ my charger cable?　　**PLUG**

11 **Use the word in capitals to form a word that fits in the gap.**

    1 Are we allowed to use _____ in the exam?   **CALCULATE**

    2 There have been some interesting _____ in computer science.   **DEVELOP**

    3 Her father is a _____ at the university.   **RESEARCH**

    4 We want to _____ young people to train for a career in computer programming.   **COURAGE**

    5 The world's first computer is now just a _____ in a museum.   **CURIOUS**

    6 Are you _____ about the future?   **OPTIMIST**

    7 The internet wasn't working, so he couldn't use the _____ printer.   **WIRE**

    8 That's the most _____ story I've ever heard. I don't believe it.   **CREDIBLE**

Writing

12 **Read the writing task and write your answer in 140–190 words in an appropriate style.**

You see an advert asking for volunteers to help at a Science and Technology fair that will be taking place in your town next summer. Write a formal email to the organiser, Ms Davis, offering to help. Give some details about your interests and experience, including any relevant activities you will be doing between now and then, or any experience you will have had by then.

Grammar

1 Complete the email with the present perfect simple or present perfect continuous form of the verbs.

> Hi Max
>
> Well, we ¹ _____ (be) here in Scotland for three days now. It's the first holiday we ² _____ (have) since 2019! Unfortunately, it ³ _____ (rain) for the past two days, and we ⁴ _____ (not leave) the hotel yet.
>
> Dad ⁵ _____ (complain) non-stop since we arrived. He just wants to go out and play golf. I don't think he'll be good at it because he ⁶ _____ (not play) for years. I ⁷ _____ (read) the latest book by my favourite author. I ⁸ _____ (not finish) it yet, but it's great.
>
> Maria ⁹ _____ (just / come) into the room. Her hair is wet because she ¹⁰ _____ (swim). At least there's an indoor pool here – so that keeps her happy. I don't know what I'm going to do when I ¹¹ _____ (finish) my book. I ¹² _____ (read) half of it already! Let's hope the weather changes soon!
>
> Best wishes
>
> Tom

2 Complete the sentences with these words. Use *a / an* where necessary.

| advice | experience | food | glass | barbecue | medicine | illness | sugar |

1 When I'm ill, I usually take _____ .
2 My parents are having _____ at the weekend.
3 She's never suffered from _____ in her life.
4 When I have a problem, I always ask my grandmother for _____ .
5 I'm hungry. I need _____ .
6 You look thirsty. Would you like _____ of water?
7 Do you like _____ in your coffee?
8 Spending a week in hospital was _____ I don't want to repeat.

3 Choose the correct option (a–c) to complete the sentences.

1 ___ work by nine o'clock?
   a Will you be starting   b Will you have started   c Shall you start
2 ___ to the cinema tonight?
   a Shall we go   b Will we have gone   c Do we go
3 Don't worry. Everything ___ OK.
   a is going to be   b will have been   c will be being
4 Do you think the match ___ yet?
   a will finish   b will be finishing   c will have finished
5 Don't play football in the house! You ___ something.
   a 'll be breaking   b 're going to break   c 'll have broken
6 How long ___ here by the end of this year?
   a will you work   b will you be working   c will you have worked
7 This time next week, we ___ .
   a 're going to sunbathe   b 'll be sunbathing   c 'll have sunbathed
8 Computers ___ more intelligent than humans soon.
   a will be   b will have been   c are being

4 Complete the sentences with the verbs using *will* or the present simple form.

1 I _____ (check) the computer for viruses before you _____ (start) using it, just to be safe.

2 The children _____ (have to) have a shower as soon as they _____ (get) back from their camping trip.

3 The moment it _____ (start) to rain, they _____ (stop) the tennis match.

4 We _____ (wait) until the weather _____ (improve), then we _____ (leave).

5 When I _____ (get) my new bike, I _____ (ride) to school every day.

6 As soon as I _____ (know) what time the train is, I _____ (tell) you if I can pick you up.

7 Jan _____ (buy) a new house when the prize money _____ (arrive).

8 They _____ (call) us the moment they _____ (hear) any news.

5 Correct the mistakes in these sentences.

1 Would you like a help with your homework?

_____

2 He's been run in the park.

_____

3 I've taken just some cough medicine.

_____

4 What time are you going deliver the pizza?

_____

5 She's been doing gymnastics since three years.

_____

6 I'll phone you after I'll make the dinner.

_____

7 They yet won't have finished.

_____

8 Let me give you an advice.

_____

6 Choose the correct option to complete the sentences.

1 I *have slept / slept* well last night.

2 Greg has been playing games *all morning / yesterday* morning.

3 Would you like *a / some* milk?

4 *Shall / Will* I walk with you to the bus stop?

5 You can go out *when / until* you've finished your homework.

6 We'll *have known / be knowing* each other for two years next week.

7 Don't call her now. She *sleeps / will be sleeping*.

8 I've made *some / any* cakes for your party.

Exam practice

7 For questions 1–8, read the text below. Use the word given in capitals at the end of each line to form a word that fits in the gap in the same line. There is an example at the beginning (0).

The urban poor

As well as being places of great (0) _economic_ wealth, big cities are places where poverty   **ECONOMY**
exists on a large scale. It is a problem for which there has not yet been found a (1) _____ .   **SOLVE**
There are, of course, poor people in country areas, but that is where the (2) _____ ends.   **SIMILAR**
The poor in urban areas are more likely to suffer from (3) _____ than the poor in rural   **ILL**
areas. The situation of the rural poor is regarded as (4) _____ because there   **AVOID**
are very few opportunities for them to improve their lives. This is not (5) _____ believed   **GENERAL**
to be the case with the urban poor, who are often blamed for the state of their own lives. Their
spirits weakened, the urban poor can begin to accept their (6) _____ conditions as their   **LIFE**
fate. Eventually, some may become susceptible to (7) _____ . Unable to face the prospect   **DEPRESS**
of a life without hope, they can face much greater (8) _____ when trying to   **DIFFICULT**
change their situation.

8 For questions 9–16, read the text below and decide which answer (A, B, C or D) best fits each gap. There is an example at the beginning (0).

Kuala Lumpur: A city of contrasts

Kuala Lumpur is the (0) __ of Malaysia and perhaps the city in Asia which has changed most in the (9) __ twenty-years. It now (10) __ a relaxed, colonial atmosphere with space age technology.

In the early 21st century, most of the business in the (11) __ was carried out in Hong Kong or Singapore. At that time Kuala Lumpur was in (12) __ of being left behind the other big far eastern cities, but nowadays it is world class. However, although remarkable progress has been (13) __ , many Malaysians still feel that the rest of the world has been slow to recognise this. With that in mind, they are always seeking to improve their standard of living by (14) __ only the very best.

However, success has brought with it certain problems. Traffic sometimes creates a deadly smog which the locals refuse to (15) __ on, and the Western media has a habit of criticising the city. (16) __ these kinds of problems, the Malaysians remain determined to reach the top.

0	**A**	leading	**B**	primary	**C**	first	**(D)**	capital
9	**A**	latest	**B**	later	**C**	last	**D**	recent
10	**A**	shares	**B**	connects	**C**	sticks	**D**	combines
11	**A**	region	**B**	territory	**C**	place	**D**	location
12	**A**	risk	**B**	danger	**C**	emergency	**D**	jeopardy
13	**A**	done	**B**	carried	**C**	made	**D**	taken
14	**A**	asking	**B**	persisting	**C**	insisting	**D**	demanding
15	**A**	mention	**B**	comment	**C**	refer	**D**	discuss
16	**A**	Despite	**B**	Although	**C**	However	**D**	But

Grammar

9 For questions 1–10 choose the word or phrase that best completes the sentence.

1 Only ___ people came to my party.
A many
B a little
C a lot of
D a few

2 Oh, there you are! I've ___ for you?
A been looking
B look
C looking
D looked

3 'Can you give me some money?'
'Sorry, I don't have ___ .'
A some
B none
C any
D few

4 He will win if he ___ fast enough.
A 'll run
B runs
C ran
D running

5 I'm not speaking to him ___ he apologises.
A when
B after
C because
D until

6 I ___ a headache pill, so I'll feel better soon.
A just have taken
B 've taken just
C just taken
D 've just taken

7 Would you like a ___ of cheese?
A jar
B piece
C loaf
D can

8 Laura looks ill. She ___ sick.
A 'll be
B 'll have been
C 'll be being
D 's going to be

9 James ___ to lunch tomorrow, isn't he?
A comes
B is coming
C will come
D has come

10 Do you think the children ___ lunch yet?
A ate
B eat
C will have eaten
D are going to eat

Vocabulary

10 For questions 11–20 choose the word or phrase that best completes the sentence.

11 This vaccination will protect you ___ the virus.
A against
B on
C over
D to

12 I need a holiday to recharge my ___ .
A brains
B legs
C device
D batteries

13 You'll lose your work if you don't back it ___ .
A off
B on
C out
D up

14 Do you want to ___ to our collection?
A focus
B contribute
C work
D intend

15 I feel really ___ the weather today.
A under
B over
C off
D by

16 Try this medicine. It'll do you the ___ of good.
A universe
B earth
C world
D planet

17 Daniel has ___ up with a brilliant plan!
A gone
B come
C run
D made

18 He ___ up an IT company eight years ago.
A worked
B had
C lifted
D set

19 Don't worry. You'll be on the ___ in no time!
A mend
B fix
C repair
D improve

20 Can I plug my charger cable ___ here?
A on
B out
C in
D off

1 Which of these sentences are correct (C) and incorrect (I)?

1 You needn't read this if you don't want to. ___
2 He ought to getting more sleep. ___
3 People can be happy and poor. ___
4 We must to try our best at all times. ___
5 She may be succeed in the world of finance. ___

6 He can't be 18! ___
7 I think she might be right. ___
8 Could you speaking a little bit louder, please? ___
9 No, you mayn't eat the last biscuit. ___
10 We were able to get tickets at the last minute.___

How many did you get right? ☐

Grammar

Modals and semi-modals

can and *could*

We use *can* + infinitive (without *to*):
- to talk about general ability in the present and the future.
*Emma **can ride** a bike.*
- for requests.
***Can** you **give** me some help?*
- for permission.
*Yes, you **can use** my laptop.*

We use *can't* + infinitive (without *to*) to show that we are sure that something isn't true.
*Mrs Smith **can't be** on holiday. I've just seen her.*

We use *could* + infinitive (without *to*):
- to talk about general ability in the past (past form of *can*).
*Oliver **could play** the piano when he was three.*
- to talk about possibility.
*He **could win** the competition.*
- for polite requests.
***Could** you **close** the door please?*
- to make suggestions.
*You **could take** extra lessons in the evening.*

may and *might*

We use *may* + infinitive (without *to*):
- to talk about possibility in the future.
*She **may decide** not to go to university.*
- for polite requests (with *I* and *we*).
***May** I **sit** here?*
- for polite permission.
*Yes, you **may bring** a friend with you.*

We use *might* + infinitive (without *to*):
- to talk about possibility in the future.
*I **might get** a job abroad.*
- as the past tense of *may*.
*She said she **might buy** an electric bike.*

must

We use *must* + infinitive (without *to*):
- to say that something is necessary.

*I **must get** some milk before the shop closes.*
- to talk about obligations.

*You **must submit** your application by 30th November.*
- to show that we are sure that something is true.

*She **must be** very happy that she passed all her exams.*
- to recommend something.

*You **must see** this film.*

We use *mustn't* + infinitive (without *to*) to talk about something that is not allowed.

*You **mustn't use** your phone in the library.*

should

We use *should* + infinitive (without *to*):
- to give advice.

*You **should do** the best you can.*
- to ask for advice.

***Should** I **apply** for this job?*

would

We use *would* + infinitive (without *to*):
- for past actions that we did regularly, but we don't do now.

*We **would** often **have** lunch in the park.*
- polite requests.

***Would** you **do** me a favour, please?*

needn't

We use *needn't* + infinitive (without *to*) to say that something is not necessary. We don't use it in affirmative sentences.

*You **needn't finish** this work tonight. Tomorrow will be fine.*

be able to

We use *be able to* to talk about:
- general ability.

*We **are able to** travel quite easily.*
- a specific ability in the past. (*Could* cannot be used here.)

*I **was able to** meet the deadline.*

have to

We use *have to*:
- to say that something is necessary.

*Do they **have to** prepare the food for the party?*
- to talk about obligation.

*We **have to** hand in our projects at the end of the week.*

mustn't and don't have to

There is an important difference between *mustn't* and *don't have to*. We use *mustn't* to say that something is not allowed, whereas we use *don't have to* to show that there is no obligation or necessity.

*You **mustn't take** photos in the museum.*

*You **don't have to** come with us to the concert. You can stay at home if you want.*

> **Note**
>
> Ought to can also be used to give advice, but it is not usually used in the question form.
> *You **ought to** study a bit harder.*

> **Note**
>
> We can also use *need* as an ordinary verb. It has affirmative, negative and question forms and it is usually used in the present simple and the past simple. It is followed by the infinitive + *to*.
> *She **needs to** try harder.*
> *He **didn't need to** hand in his essay today.*
> *Do we **need to** get anything from the market?*

9

Grammar exercises

2 **Choose the correct option to complete the sentences.**

1 I'm glad I *can / was able to* speak to you before you left.
2 *Can I / Am I able* to help you with anything?
3 She'd love to *can / be able to* work in a theatre.
4 *Can / Could* you hear the cats fighting outside last night?
5 Fortunately, my parents *can / were able to* buy their own house just before I was born.
6 Our hotel was beautiful, and we *can / could* see the whole city from our window.
7 No, sorry. You *can't / aren't able* to borrow my laptop – I need it.
8 *Could you / Were you able* to finish the work in class?

3 **Complete the sentences with *must, mustn't* or *don't / doesn't have to*.**

1 Sam _____ wear uniform at his school. He can wear any clothes he likes.
2 You _____ be late, or you will be in trouble.
3 All students _____ complete their projects by 6th April.
4 My grandparents _____ travel far to visit us – they only live around the corner.
5 You _____ bring animals into the hospital. It's not allowed.
6 The law in the UK says that motorcyclists _____ always wear a helmet when riding.
7 Students _____ wear football boots in the gym. Only trainers are allowed.
8 You _____ get up early tomorrow. You can stay in bed all day if you feel like it!

4 **Complete the sentences with *can't be* or *must be*.**

1 Dan _____ at home. I've knocked and there's no answer.
2 That café _____ very good. There's never anyone in it!
3 No one has bought that house yet. It _____ too expensive.
4 It _____ a great show, because it's impossible to get tickets for it!
5 That _____ Andrea at the door – she's still in Germany.
6 Sara _____ ill, because she isn't at school and she hates missing lessons.

5 **Choose the correct option (a–c) to complete the sentences.**

1 ___ I ask you a personal question?
   a Must   b May   c Needn't

2 Tim ___ write his name until he was six.
   a couldn't   b can't   c mustn't

3 It ___ be easy to work 12 hours a day, seven days a week.
   a shouldn't   b can't   c mustn't

4 You ___ succeed if you work hard enough.
   a can't   b must   c might

5 She ___ be very clever to go to university at the age of 16.
   a must   b can   c should

6 People ___ leave litter in the park – it's not fair on others.
   a couldn't   b might not   c shouldn't

7 Burglars ___ to get in through a window last night.
   a can   b could   c were able

8 You ___ worry about your future. I'm sure you'll be successful.
   a can't   b needn't   c couldn't

6 Complete the conversations with these modal verbs.

A | can | can't | don't have to | might | mustn't | should |

Judy: I'm worried about Tom. It's 10 p.m. and he isn't home yet. What [1] _____ I do?

Robert: You [2] _____ worry, I'm sure he's fine. He [3] _____ be at Sophie's house – have you phoned her?

Judy: He [4] _____ be at Sophie's house. She's in France with her family.

Robert: Oh.

Judy: [5] _____ I borrow your phone? I want to call his friend, Mark.

Robert: It's OK. You [6] _____ borrow my phone. Here he comes now!

B | can | can't | couldn't | might | must | shouldn't |

Joel: Look, Mum. I [1] _____ do tricks on my skateboard.

Sarah: Be careful, Joel – you [2] _____ jump so high – you [3] _____ hurt yourself.

Simon: He [4] _____ be very talented. I [5] _____ do tricks like that when I was his age.

Sarah: I don't know where his talent comes from. It [6] _____ be me – I'm no good at things like that.

7 Complete the sentences with one word in each gap.

1 I'll _____ to buy a new swimming costume before we go on holiday.
2 You _____ not speak during the test, or you'll be asked to leave.
3 I always go to my aunt for advice. She tells me what I _____ do.
4 We don't have _____ go to school today. It's the holidays!
5 When Mo was a little boy, he _____ able to run for miles without getting tired.
6 Mum _____ to work late last night; she didn't get home until midnight.
7 My careers advisor thinks I _____ to consider studying Law.
8 He _____ not want us to come and visit him, so call him first.

Vocabulary

Prepositions

8 Complete the phrases with these prepositions. Some prepositions can be used more than once.

| at | in | of | to |

1 according _____
2 be good _____
3 be surprised _____
4 dream _____

5 make a success _____
6 spread _____
7 take advantage _____
8 take part _____

9 Complete the sentences with the phrases from Exercise 8.

1 _____ researchers, rich people are not much happier than poor people.
2 If you work hard enough, you'll _____ anything you do.
3 I was very _____ the success of the chess club. I didn't expect it to be so popular.
4 When I was a child, I used to _____ being an astronaut.
5 Last week, our whole class _____ a programming workshop with a computer scientist.
6 The reason I don't like basketball is because I'm not very _____ it.
7 The virus quickly _____ every computer on the network.
8 I'm going to _____ this online photography course – it's free.

9

Exam practice

10 Complete the second sentence so that it has a similar meaning to the first sentence, using the word given. Do not change the word given. You must use between two and five words.

1 It isn't necessary for you to post your application. You can submit it online.

You _____ your application. You can submit it online.   **HAVE**

2 Playing football is not allowed here.

You _____ here.   **MUSTN'T**

3 I'm sure Noah isn't at school today.

Noah _____ today.   **BE**

4 It is possible that it'll rain tomorrow.

It _____ tomorrow.   **MIGHT**

5 It wasn't necessary for him to bring his own guitar.

He _____ his own guitar.   **HAVE**

6 I advise you to talk to someone who's already doing that job.

You _____ someone who's already doing that job.   **OUGHT**

7 I hope you have a successful time at university.

I hope _____ your time at university.   **MAKE**

8 I hope it's possible for me to participate in the drama workshop.

I hope I _____ in the drama workshop.   **PART**

Word formation

11 Use the word in capitals to form a word that fits in the gap.

1 I was surprised by the teacher's _____ request.   USUAL

2 We're planning to have a big _____ when we finish all our exams.   CELEBRATE

3 He _____ completed the course.   SUCCEED

4 What do you think is your greatest _____ ?   ACHIEVE

5 My cousin is very _____ . He's planning to start his own marketing business.   AMBITION

6 Ella is _____ to get a job as an aircraft engineer.   DETERMINE

7 Although she was a successful businesswoman, everyone was impressed by her _____ .   MODEST

8 His only ambition is to be _____ before he gets old.   WEALTH

Writing

12 What are the rules? In your notebook, write some rules for your perfect school. Write:

- three things that students have to do
- three things that students don't have to do
- three things that students mustn't do.

Unit 10

1 **Which of these sentences are correct (C) and incorrect (I)?**

1 Simon should have tried harder. ___
2 My company could have been successful. ___
3 I would helped you if I could. ___
4 Should I invited Tim to the party? ___
5 They might left earlier. ___

6 That must have been a difficult decision. ___
7 You can't have finish already! ___
8 Could Megan have been upset about her results? ___
9 I needn't have sold my bike. ___
10 You could have succeed if you had tried. ___

How many did you get right? ☐

Grammar

Perfect modals

may / might have

We use *may / might have* + past participle to show that we are not sure about something in the past.
*They **may have heard** the news already.*

should have

We use *should have* + past participle:
- to show that something we were expecting did not happen.
*James **should have arrived** at his interview by now.*
- to criticise our own or someone else's behaviour.
*You **shouldn't have tried** to climb on the roof!*

could have

We use *could have* + past participle:
- to show that we are not sure about something in the past.
*I **could have left** my keys in my gym bag.*
- to say that something was possible in the past, but that it didn't happen.
*She **could have been** an actor, but she became a teacher instead.*

can't / couldn't have

We use *can't / couldn't have* + past participle to show that we are sure that something is not true about the past.
*Dan **can't have won** the gold medal – he isn't fast enough.*

must have

We use *must have* + past participle to show that we are sure that something is true about the past.
*You **must have been** happy when they offered you the job.*

would have

We use *would have* + past participle to say that we were willing to do something, but that we didn't do it.
*I **would have lent** him the money, but he didn't ask me.*

needn't have

We use *needn't have* + past participle to say it wasn't necessary to do something but you did it anyway.
*You **needn't have rushed**. The interviews are running about 20 minutes late.*

10

Grammar exercises

2 **Choose the correct option to complete the sentences.**

1 I think I might *have* / *had* forgotten to close the windows.
2 You *could* / *must* have won that prize if you had bought a ticket.
3 Sam *shouldn't* / *mustn't* have spoken to me like that.
4 She *can* / *can't* have finished her work already.
5 Oh dear, I think I *would* / *might* have made a mistake.
6 We *could* / *must* have gone with them, but we didn't feel like it.
7 The car is not here – it *can* / *must* have been stolen.
8 We all did the wrong homework, so the teacher *mustn't* / *couldn't* have explained it clearly.
9 *Would* / *Should* you have preferred to have studied a different subject at university?
10 He *can't* / *mustn't* have forgotten his lunch money again!

3 **Use the prompts to write sentences.**

1 studied / might / She / at school / German / have

_____

2 may / received / not / Simon / have / his invitation

_____

3 a great idea / That / been / not / have / might

_____

4 late home / We / be / may / tonight

_____

5 become / have / She / a famous singer / might

_____

6 may / an accident / There / been / have

_____

7 not / Jane / ready / been / have / might

_____

8 gone / to the library / He / already / may / have

_____

4 **Complete the email with these modals verbs and the verbs in brackets.**

can't	might	must	should	shouldn't	would

Dear Ben

Congratulations on passing all your exams this year. You ¹ _____ (be) delighted when you found out!

Unfortunately, Evie didn't do as well as you. She ² _____ (study) harder, in my opinion, and she ³ _____ (go) out with her friends every night! She's a clever girl, and I'm certain she ⁴ _____ (pass) if she'd tried harder.

She's still upset. It ⁵ _____ (be) easy for her when she heard that you had passed them all. I'm hoping that she ⁶ _____ (learn) her lesson now, and will work really hard next year.

Love

Aunt Becky

5 Complete the sentences with *can't have* or *must have* and the past participle of the verbs.

1 He _____ (know) the answer to the question, because he left it blank.

2 You look tired – you _____ (go) to bed late last night!

3 They _____ (enjoy) their meal because they only ate half of it.

4 You _____ (forget) to invite Tanya to the party, because she says she didn't know about it.

5 Katy said the exam was really easy. She _____ (study) a lot for it.

6 It _____ (be) Mrs Green who you saw in town, because she moved away last year.

7 Ted _____ (steal) the money. He's a very honest boy.

8 Someone _____ (call) a taxi because there's one waiting outside.

6 Complete the sentences with *should* have or *shouldn't have.*

1 You didn't wait for me.
You *should have waited for me* _____ .

2 He lied to us.
He _____ .

3 She broke her promise.
She _____ .

4 We didn't say thank you to you.
We _____ .

5 I was late for my piano lesson.
I _____ .

6 My uncle didn't buy my aunt a birthday present.
My uncle _____ .

7 The boys ate too much chocolate cake.
The boys _____ .

8 She didn't apologise.
She _____ .

7 Write sentences with *needn't have.*

1 You brought flowers! That wasn't necessary.
You *needn't have brought flowers* _____ .

2 We went shopping for food. We already had plenty.
We _____ .

3 He called to say he was late. I already knew that.
He _____ .

4 I got up early this morning. There was nothing to do.
I _____ .

5 She studied hard, but the exam was easy.
She _____ .

6 They were worried. There was nothing to worry about.
They _____ .

7 I gave her my umbrella. It didn't rain.
I _____ .

8 Charlie took the medicine. It didn't make him better.
Charlie _____ .

10

Vocabulary

Collocations and expressions

8 Complete the table with these words and phrases.

| a business | a difference | advice | an impression | confidence |
| experience | someone a chance | understanding | | |

BUILD	_____	_____
GAIN	_____	_____
GIVE	_____	_____
MAKE	_____	_____

9 Complete the sentences with these words.

| break | fire | places | record | sights | storm |

1 James has set his _____ on becoming a film producer, and I'm sure he'll succeed.
2 After the band's appearance at a big festival, they're really going _____ .
3 The charity has a strong track _____ of acting fast in emergencies.
4 The business lost money in its first year, so the second year will be make or _____ .
5 The money we made in the café in summer should help us weather the _____ of the winter months.
6 Lucy has come up with so many ideas for inventions that I'm sure one of them will set the world on _____ .

Exam practice

Sentence transformation

10 Complete the second sentence so that it has a similar meaning to the first sentence, using the word given. Do not change the word given. You must use between two and five words

1 Perhaps Amy went to the park.

   Amy _____ to the park. **COULD**

2 It's a pity you didn't ask for her autograph.

   You _____ for her autograph. **SHOULD**

3 It was wrong of him to shout at the children.

   He _____ at the children. **SHOUTED**

4 Maybe Amelie didn't want to be in the play.

   Amelie _____ to be in the play. **MIGHT**

5 We worried unnecessarily about the weather.

   We _____ about the weather. **NEEDN'T**

6 I'm going to wear smart clothes for the interview because I want them to remember me positively.

   I'm going to wear smart clothes for the interview because I want to

   _____ . **MAKE**

7 I had a ticket, but I didn't want to go to the show.

   I _____ to the show, but I didn't want to. **COULD**

8 Harry looks happy, so I think his team won the championship.

   Harry's team _____ , because he looks happy. **MUST**

Open cloze

11 Read the sentences and think of a word which best fits each gap. Use only one word in each gap.

1 He works for a local charity because he wants to _____ a difference in his community.

2 They might _____ forgotten there's no school today.

3 I think my bike might have _____ stolen.

4 It can take a long time and a lot of hard work to _____ a business.

5 The kids must have _____ a great time at the fair.

6 Sophie was delighted when they _____ her a chance to lead the research expedition.

7 Can you _____ me some advice on starting my own business?

8 He _____ have gone to work if he could, but he was too ill.

Writing

12 Read the writing task and write your answer in 140–190 words in an appropriate style.

In your English class you have been talking about success and teacher wants you to write an essay. Write an essay using all the notes and giving reasons for your point of view.

Exam results are the best measure of success at school. Do you agree?

Write about:

- what exam results show
- other measures of success
- a specific example.

Awareness

1 **Which of these sentences are correct (C) and incorrect (I)?**

1 They had just started eaten when the
   doorbell rang.   ___

2 We had forgotten to put petrol in the car.   ___

3 Mandy had been waiting since an hour
   and a half.   ___

4 Had the children been fighting?   ___

5 The archaeologist had been found
   something amazing.   ___

6 I wanted to go because it had been great
   fun last time.   ___

7 She was tired because she had running.   ___

8 I was surprised that you hadn't been
   hearing the story before.   ___

9 They hadn't seen the first film, so it was
   hard to understand the second.   ___

10 We had been playing computer games
    for about nine o'clock that morning.   ___

How many did you get right? ☐

Grammar

Past perfect simple

Affirmative	Negative	Questions
I / He / She / It / We / You / They **had ('d) lived**.	I / He / She / It / We / You / They **had not (hadn't) lived**.	**Had** I / he / she / it / we / you / they **lived**?
Short Answers		
Yes, I / he / she / it / we / you / they **had**.	**No**, I / he / she / it / we / you /they **hadn't**.	

Spelling: climb → climb**ed**, love → lov**ed**, travel → travel**led**, study → stud**ied**, play → play**ed**

> **Note**
> Some verbs are irregular and do not follow these spelling rules. See a list of irregular verbs and their past participles on pages 145–146.

We use the past perfect simple for an action or situation that finished before another action, situation or time in the past.
*They **had read** the book **before they watched** the film.*
***By the time she was** ten, she **had decided** to study archaeology.*

> **Note**
> Some common time expressions that are often used with the past perfect simple are *already, for, for a long time / ages, just, never, once, since 2019 / July, so far, yet*, etc.
> *I hadn't played a guitar **for weeks** because of my broken finger.*

Past perfect continuous

Affirmative	Negative	Questions
I / He / She / It / We / You / They **had ('d) been** living.	I / He / She / It / We / You / They **had not (hadn't) been** living.	**Had** I / he / she / it / we / you / they **been** living?
Short Answers		
Yes, I / he / she / it / we / you / they **had.**	**No**, I / he / she / it / we / you / they **hadn't.**	

Spelling: make → ma**king**, run → ru**nning**, ti**dy** → ti**dying**

We use the past perfect continuous:

- for actions that started in the past and were still in progress when another action started or when something happened.

*I **had been sleeping** for about four hours when the alarm went off.*

- for actions that continued over a period of time in the past and had an effect on a later action.

*Sarah was confident about her exams because she **had been studying** for months.*

> **Note**
>
> Some common time expressions that are often used with the past perfect continuous are *all day / night / week, for years / a long time / ages, since*. We can use *How long ...?* with the past perfect continuous in questions and *for (very) long* in questions and negative sentences.
> *I'**d been trying all week** to get in touch with Amy.*
> *__Had__ they __been thinking__ about visiting the Mayan ruins __for long__?*

Grammar exercises

2 **Choose the correct option to complete the sentences.**

1 The archaeologists *had dug / had been digging* at the site for three months.

2 As soon as I saw his face, I knew he *had won / had been winning* the match.

3 Simon *had tried / had been trying* to find his wallet all morning.

4 They had never *seen / been seeing* such a beautiful painting.

5 After we *had eaten / had been eating*, we went out into the garden.

6 How long had you *sat / been sitting* in the waiting room before the doctor saw you?

7 Had you ever *ridden / been riding* a horse before you arrived at Polk Farm?

8 My shoes were dirty because I *had walked / had been walking* in muddy fields.

9 He *hadn't saved / hadn't been saving* money for long, but he already had £50.

10 We *had known / had been knowing* each other for years.

3 **Match the beginnings of the sentences (1–8) with the endings (a–h).**

1	They had been waiting at the station	a	the match had already started.
2	Ana was in a bad mood	b	before Dad started complaining about the heat.
3	By the time we got to the stadium,	c	for two hours before the train arrived.
4	As soon as he had got permission to go,	d	he went.
5	Oscar and Max weren't talking to each other	e	because they had been fighting earlier.
6	We hadn't been on the beach for long	f	because she hadn't slept well the night before.
7	I was very excited about Sam's surprise party	g	so they weren't hungry at dinner time.
8	The kids had been eating snacks all afternoon	h	because I had never been to one before.

4 Complete the sentences with the past perfect simple or past perfect continuous form of the verbs.

1 By the time I got home last night, everyone _____ (eat) their dinner.

2 We _____ (sail) for most of the afternoon when the weather suddenly changed.

3 The man was angry because he _____ (wait) to be served for nearly an hour.

4 By 1 p.m., Stephanie _____ (ride) for six hours, and she was exhausted.

5 I was very hungry by ten o'clock because I _____ (not have) any breakfast.

6 Until yesterday, the children _____ (never see) a dolphin before.

7 Wendy was pleased because she _____ (find) her dream job.

8 How long _____ (you / hide) under the bed before Sally finally found you?

5 Choose the correct option (a–c) to complete the sentences.

1 What had he been doing ___ he hurt himself?

   a before   **b** as soon as   **c** just

2 ___ I had shut the door, I realised the key was still inside.

   a While   **b** As soon as   **c** Until

3 We had been working ___ five o'clock in the morning.

   a for   **b** when   **c** since

4 ___ had the twins been arguing for?

   a What time   **b** How long   **c** When

5 I had ___ seen the film.

   a yet   **b** always   **c** already

6 They had been looking for a new flat ___ three weeks.

   a for   **b** when   **c** since

7 She had ___ got to sleep when her phone rang.

   a yet   **b** still   **c** just

8 He had been climbing for three days, but he ___ hadn't reached the mountain top.

   a yet   **b** still   **c** just

6 Write questions for the answers.

1 _____

They had been to the museum.

2 _____

We had asked the teacher the question three times.

3 _____

No, he hadn't been invited to the meeting.

4 _____

I had been trying to phone him for two hours.

5 _____

I had been studying in the library.

6 _____

I had been there twice before.

7 _____

He had found it the previous week.

8 _____

Yes, she had been exploring the site all morning.

7 Read the situations. Then complete the sentences with the past perfect simple or past perfect continuous form of the verbs.

1 He finished his meal. Then he went upstairs to bed.

After _____ , he went upstairs to bed.

2 Sarah got a job in a café. Three weeks later the café closed.

Sarah _____ for three weeks when it closed.

3 Katy read the book. Then she lent it to me.

When _____ , she lent it to me.

4 The two teams started playing. Ten minutes later it began to snow.

The two teams _____ when _____ .

5 I phoned my mum. Before that I had a guitar lesson.

I _____ after _____ a guitar lesson.

6 She waited for half an hour. Then she realised she was in the wrong place.

She _____ before _____ .

Vocabulary

Phrasal verbs

8 Match the phrasal verbs (1–8) with their meanings (a–h).

1	ask around	☐	a	become extinct or disappear
2	burn down	☐	b	give knowledge to a younger generation
3	date back to	☐	c	discourage
4	die out	☐	d	become quickly successful
5	dig up	☐	e	speak to several different people to try and get some information
6	pass down	☐	f	come from a time in the past
7	put off	☐	g	remove something from the ground
8	take off	☐	h	destroy something, usually a building, with fire

9 Complete the sentences with the phrasal verbs from Exercise 8.

1 I was _____ the idea of visiting the ruins because someone told me the journey was very uncomfortable.

2 Traditional skills, such as jewellery making, have been _____ through the generations.

3 The dinosaurs _____ before the beginning of the Ice Age.

4 Why don't you _____ to see if anyone has lost a wallet?

5 Historians think the palace _____ the 13th century.

6 The houses were made of wood, so the fire _____ them _____ quickly.

7 Archaeologists have _____ some amazing things in the Sahara desert.

8 He invented a new computer game but unfortunately it didn't really _____ .

Exam practice

Sentence transformation

10 Complete the second sentence so that it has a similar meaning to the first sentence, using the word given. Do not change the word given. You must use between two and five words.

1 I've decided not to do this homework until tomorrow morning.

I _____ this homework until tomorrow morning. **GOING**

2 After breakfast, we went to the park.

We went to the park _____ breakfast.   **EATEN**

3 I got to the party too late to hear the band.

By the time I got to the party, _____ playing.   **STOPPED**

4 She finished using the laptop and then gave it to me.

She gave me the laptop _____ finished using it.   **SOON**

5 It was the saddest song I had ever heard.

I _____ a sadder song.   **NEVER**

6 Jake went to sleep, then his parents came home an hour later.

Jake _____ an hour when his parents came home.   **SLEEPING**

7 They didn't want to go hiking in the mountains because of the rain.

The rain _____ in the mountains.   **PUT**

8 Throughout history, many languages have disappeared.

Throughout history, many languages _____ .   **OUT**

Multiple-choice cloze

11 **Read the sentences and decide which answer (A, B, C or D) best fits each gap.**

1 No one ___ seen Mark all day, and they were getting worried about him.

   A have   **B** had   **C** has   **D** having

2 My feet hurt because I had ___ walking for hours.

   A be   **B** was   **C** been   **D** being

3 We went to bed as ___ as we had drunk our hot chocolate.

   A soon   **B** when   **C** just   **D** time

4 I hadn't heard that song for ___ .

   A time   **B** ages   **C** far   **D** never

5 The accident I had last year ___ me off climbing for life.

   A made   **B** took   **C** showed   **D** put

6 My dad has been doing the housework all ___ .

   A time   **B** long   **C** since   **D** morning

7 This recipe was ___ down from my gran to my dad to me.

   A put   **B** taken   **C** passed   **D** burned

8 He had been working there ___ 2001.

   A for   **B** since   **C** while   **D** when

Writing

12 **Write sentences in your notebook using the past perfect simple and continuous. Say what you, your family and friends had done by 2020. What had you / they been doing by that time, and for how long?**

By 2020 I had learned to ride a bike / been playing football for ten years.

Awareness

1 Which of these sentences are correct (C) and incorrect (I)?

1 Everyone is very excited, isn't he?   ___
2 I hope you didn't hurt you.   ___
3 Someone has been eating my sandwiches.   ___
4 Is this yours torch?   ___
5 No one told me about that.   ___

6 Help yourself to a drink.   ___
7 Did they meet anyone when they were away?   ___
8 Anything has been done about this yet.   ___
9 They love their new house.   ___
10 Don't touch that. It's mine!   ___

How many did you get right? ☐

Grammar

Question tags

Question tags are short questions at the end of a positive or negative sentence. They are formed with a modal or an auxiliary verb + a personal pronoun.

We usually use an affirmative question tag after a negative sentence, and a negative question tag after an affirmative sentence.
He has been to Mexico, hasn't he?
They can't come tomorrow, can they?

When the main sentence has an auxiliary verb, we use the same auxiliary in the question tag.
You haven't been to that exhibition yet, have you?
They're learning Latin, aren't they?
She was doing a research project last summer, wasn't she?

When the main sentence has a modal verb, we use the same modal verb in the question tag.
I can finish this tomorrow, can't I?
We shouldn't believe everything we read, should we?
They'll meet us at the station, won't they?

When an affirmative sentence contains a verb in the present simple or the past simple we use *do / does, don't / doesn't* and *did / didn't* in the question tag.
You enjoy learning about the past, don't you?
He didn't arrive on time, did he?

We use question tags when we want:
• someone to agree with what we are saying.
That was a brave thing to do, wasn't it?
• to make sure that what we are saying is right.
It's your turn now, isn't it?

Note

Some question tags are irregular. Notice the way these tags are formed.
I'm late, aren't I?
Nobody is ill, are they?
Let's go on a boat trip, shall we?
Don't take photos with a flash, will you?
Remember your tickets, won't you?
Be quiet, won't you?
This / That's my seat, isn't it?
These / Those vases are amazing, aren't they?

Reflexive pronouns

Subject pronoun	Reflexive pronoun
I	myself
you	yourself
he	himself
she	herself
it	itself
we	ourselves
you	yourselves
they	themselves

We use reflexive pronouns:
- when the subject and the object of the sentence are the same.

*She taught **herself** to speak Italian.*
- with some verbs (*behave, blame, cut, enjoy, help, hurt,* etc.).

*Don't blame **yourself** – it wasn't your fault.*
- when we want to emphasise that someone does something alone or without another person's help. We often use the word *by*.

*They designed the model **themselves**.*
*He walked home **by himself**.*

Indefinite pronouns

An indefinite pronoun refers to one or more unspecified people, things or places.

We use *someone, somebody, something* and *somewhere* to talk about an unspecified person, thing or place in affirmative sentences.
***Someone** left their keys in the lock.*
*I think the document must be **somewhere** in the attic.*

We use *anyone, anybody, anything* and *anywhere* to talk about an unspecified person, thing or place in negative sentences and questions.
*I can't see **anybody** in the park at the moment.*
*Have you had **anything** to eat?*

We use *everyone, everybody, everything* and *everywhere* to talk about all unspecified people, things or places. They take a singular verb.
***Everyone** enjoyed the documentary.*
*I've seen those posters **everywhere** recently.*

We use *no one, nobody, nothing* and *nowhere* with a negative meaning in affirmative sentences.
***Nobody** spoke to me.* (There wasn't anyone who spoke to me.)
*There **is nothing** we can do about it.* (We can't do anything about it.)

Possessive pronouns

Subject pronoun	Possessive adjective	Possessive pronoun
I	my	mine
you	your	ours
he	his	his
she	her	hers
it	its	-
we	our	ours
you	your	yours
they	their	theirs

We use possessive pronouns to show that something belongs to someone. Possessive pronouns replace a possessive adjective and a noun, or the possessive form and a noun.
*That's **my bag**. It's **mine**.*
*This is **Rob's calculator**. It's **his**.*
*This is **our dog**. He's **ours**.*

Grammar exercises

2 Match the beginnings of the sentences (1–8) with the endings (a–h).

1 They enjoyed the film, ☐   a   won't we?
2 There isn't any cake left, ☐   b   does it?
3 Let's watch the Olympics, ☐   c   aren't I?
4 You never arrive on time, ☐   d   has he?
5 We'll be OK, ☐   e   didn't they?
6 He's never enjoyed history, ☐   f   shall we?
7 It doesn't look very interesting, ☐   g   is there?
8 I'm in your group, ☐   h   do you?

3 Complete the questions with question tags.

1 They are going to Pompeii, _____ ?
2 Be careful, _____ ?
3 Don't forget to phone me, _____ ?
4 That looks a bit dangerous, _____ ?
5 These sandwiches aren't very nice, _____ ?
6 He lost his rucksack yesterday, _____ ?
7 Let's eat, _____ ?
8 Nobody's coming, _____ ?

4 Choose the correct option to complete the sentences.

1 Shall I help *you / yourself* with that, or can you do it *you / yourself*?
2 I told *her / herself* she was going to hurt *her / herself*.
3 Did the kids enjoy *them / themselves* yesterday? I haven't seen *them / themselves* since last week.
4 You had better fix *it / itself* soon because it's not going to fix *it / itself*.
5 No, I didn't go to the cinema by *me / myself* – Anna came with *me / myself*.
6 He didn't behave *him / himself*, so they threw *him / himself* out of the team.
7 Please help *you / yourselves* to anything in the fridge. I bought it all for *you / yourselves*.
8 How long had we been taking photos of *us / ourselves* before your mum called *us / ourselves* for dinner?

5 Complete the text with *something, somewhere, someone, anything, anywhere, anyone, everywhere, everyone, nothing, nowhere* or *no one*.

Dad was feeling sad because [1] _____ had come into his for days. 'Where is
[2] _____ ?' he asked.

'I don't think [3] _____ has got much money to spend, Jim,' Mum told him. 'It's the same
[4] _____ .'

'Well, we have to do [5] _____ to encourage people to come in and buy our things.'

'I know [6] _____ who can help,' Mum replied. That's when she called me.

'What do you want me to do?' I asked. 'I'm only 12! I can't do [7] _____ .'

'Sit down, Jack,' said Mum. 'There's [8] _____ to worry about. I just want you to put
[9] _____ on and go [10] _____ with it.'

'I don't want to go [11] _____ !'

Then mum brought out a big sign and hung it around my neck. The sign said 'COME TO JIM'S

SHOP – [12] _____ IN TOWN IS CHEAPER!

6 Choose the correct option to complete the sentences.

1 I've got a dog. *Its / Their* name is Rufus.
2 *Our / Ours* house is quite big.
3 This isn't *your / yours* book. It's *my / mine*.
4 I left *my / mine* laptop at home.
5 Tom has forgotten his pen. Can he use *your / yours*?
6 I didn't know Emilia was *your / yours* cousin.
7 That bike doesn't belong to me. It's *her / hers*.
8 *Their / Theirs* parents have bought *our / ours* car. It's *their / theirs* now!

7 Choose the correct option (a–c) to complete the sentences.

1 Don't forget you've got a test tomorrow, ___ ?
  a have you   b will you   c do you
2 There's ___ on TV tonight.
  a nothing   b nowhere   c anything
3 Is this ___ phone?
  a yours   b your   c you
4 Ouch! I've just cut ___ .
  a me   b my   c myself
5 Let's go to the cinema this evening, ___ ?
  a shall we   b will we   c don't we
6 I've looked for my wallet, but I can't find it ___ .
  a anywhere   b somewhere   c everywhere

Vocabulary

Word formation

8 Match the words (1–8) with their meanings (a–h).

1 analyse   a say or do again
2 conclude   b something that you think of or remember
3 origin   c how much something is worth
4 prove   d carefully examine something
5 repeat   e show that something is true
6 research   f the cause or starting point of something
7 thought   g study something carefully
8 value   h decide something after examining or studying it

9 Use the word in capitals to form a word that fits in the gap.

1 I don't like this kind of music – it's too _____ . **REPEAT**
2 There is no _____ that Mr Norris committed the crime. **PROVE**
3 I'd love to work as a _____ on a historical site. **RESEARCH**
4 The scientists did an _____ of the chemicals. **ANALYSE**
5 Be careful with that plate – it's very _____ . **VALUE**
6 You look very _____ – what are you thinking about? **THOUGHT**
7 The palace was _____ quite small, but a lot of rooms were added later. **ORIGIN**
8 Did you come to any _____ about this? **CONCLUDE**

Exam practice

Sentence transformation

10 **Complete the second sentence so that it has a similar meaning to the first sentence, using the word given. Do not change the word given. You must use between two and five words.**

1 Please put down that bag – it belongs to me.
That bag _____ , so please put it down.　　　　**IS**

2 The children didn't have any help cooking the dinner this evening.
The children _____ this evening.　　　　**THEMSELVES**

3 I think my pen was stolen.
I think _____ pen.　　　　**SOMEONE**

4 I heard that the exhibition was enjoyed by all the people who went.
I heard _____ the exhibition.　　　　**EVERYONE**

5 Nothing has been done about the broken window.
Nobody _____ about the broken window.　　　　**ANYTHING**

6 Is this notebook yours?
Is _____ notebook?　　　　**YOUR**

7 I hope he has fun at the water park.
I hope _____ at the water park.　　　　**HIMSELF**

8 No one taught her to play chess.
She _____ chess.　　　　**HERSELF**

Open cloze

11 **Read the sentences and think of a word which best fits each gap. Use only one word in each gap.**

1 That car belongs to us. It's _____ .
2 You don't want to go home yet, _____ you?
3 I didn't speak to _____ at the party.
4 They can't find _____ shoes.
5 Don't come home too late, _____ you?
6 Sam must be hiding _____ , but we can't find him.
7 That wasn't very clever, _____ it?
8 I've had no help with this – I had to do it by _____ .

Writing

12 **Read the writing task and write your answer in 140–190 words in an appropriate style.**

You have received an email from your English-speaking friend Katy. She would like to hear about a trip you have recently returned from. Write an email to her telling her about:

• someone you met on the trip
• something funny that happened on the trip
• somewhere you'll never forget.

Grammar

1 Choose the correct options to complete the conversation.

Donna: Katy, are you going into town this afternoon?

Katy: I'm not sure. I *must / might* go if I have time.

Donna: *Could / Shall* you buy me the latest copy of Rock Magazine if you do go?

Katy: OK. But you *must / may* pay me back that £3 you owe me first.

Donna: Oh, I forgot about that. Sorry, I won't *be able to / could* pay you back until tomorrow.

Katy: That's fine. You *mustn't / don't have* to pay me today – but you *mustn't / don't have* forget tomorrow!

Donna: I *won't / don't*.

Katy: You *ought / should* keep a note of how much money you owe people.

Donna: You're right. *Might / Would* you buy me a notebook and pen as well?

2 Complete the sentences with *might have, should have, shouldn't have, can't have, must have, would have* or *needn't have* and the verbs.

1 I _____ (win) the lottery because I never buy a ticket.

2 We're not sure where Jack is – he _____ (go) to the library with Harry.

3 You _____ (buy) that car when you had the chance – you'll never get a better deal.

4 It turned out that we _____ (run) to the station, because the train was 15 minutes late.

5 I'm sure Jo _____ (come) to meet you if you had asked her.

6 Mia _____ (speak) so rudely to the teacher. She's in trouble now!

7 Have you finished your dinner already? You _____ (be) very hungry!

8 Where's Ben? He _____ (arrive) by now.

3 Complete the sentences with the past perfect simple or past perfect continuous form of the verbs.

1 After we _____ (visit) the Parthenon, we went for lunch.

2 They _____ (walk) in the mountains for about two hours when the thunderstorm began.

3 My feet were sore because I _____(run).

4 When she _____ (do) all the shopping, she bought herself a cup of coffee.

5 It was obvious that the baby _____ (cry) for quite a long time.

6 He was late because he _____ (not realise) that the motorway was closed.

7 The teacher knew when she entered the classroom that the students _____ (not behave) themselves.

8 I was sure I _____ (see) her face somewhere before.

4 Choose the correct option to complete the sentences.

1 You *can't / needn't* worry about Freddie. He'll be fine.

2 We *had been knowing / had known* for years about the secret.

3 Everyone is very tired, *isn't they / aren't they*?

4 I don't know *anybody / nobody* here.

5 Is this coat *you / yours*?

6 You're lucky – you *could / must* have been badly injured.

7 Do we *must / need* to do this test again?

8 How long *had they waited / had they been waiting* before the meal arrived?

5 Choose the correct option (a–c) to complete the sentences.

1 I couldn't find my bag ___ .

   a anywhere   b nowhere   c everywhere

2 Did you hurt ___ when you fell?

   a you   b your   c yourself

3 Is this yours or is it ___ ?

   a me   b my   c mine

4 You can do this, ___ ?

   a can you   b can't you   c could you

5 ___ is knocking on the door.

   a Anyone   b Someone   c Anything

6 The children are playing by ___ .

   a themselves   b them   c theirs

7 That's not his problem, it's ___ .

   a her   b hers   c herself

8 She wouldn't have enjoyed it, ___ ?

   a would she   b will she   c wouldn't she

9 We entertained ___ by telling each other stories.

   a us   b ours   c ourselves

10 Don't tell anyone, ___ ?

   a do you   b won't you   c will you

6 Correct the mistakes in these sentences.

1 You really ought exercise more.

_____

2 Should I told you earlier?

_____

3 We had been waiting in line since ten minutes.

_____

4 Don't blame you about it.

_____

5 We forgotten to do our homework.

_____

6 I would asked her if I'd had the courage.

_____

7 Could you being a bit quieter please?

_____

8 That must have being an exciting day!

_____

Exam practice

7 For questions 1–8, read the text below and think of a word which best fits each gap. Use only one word in each gap. There is an example at the beginning (0).

A costly mistake

In a court of law, the prosecution **(0)** ___*has*___ to prove that a person is guilty before he or she can be punished. However, this is not the case outside the legal system.

David Jones and his wife, Paula, were thrilled when a friend suggested that David should apply **(1)** _____ a job in the international company he worked for. He did so, but was puzzled when the company put his interview **(2)** _____ several times. When he asked his friend **(3)** _____ this had happened, he got no answer.

Paula wanted to find out why the company **(4)** _____ acted this way, so she went to see an uncle who was a police officer. He eventually told her that someone had reported seeing a car with the same registration number **(5)** _____ her husband's car being driven away **(6)** _____ the scene of a crime. This information had **(7)** _____ put on a computer file to which the company had access. At the time of the crime David was abroad, so obviously a mistake had been **(8)** _____ . Nevertheless, the Joneses could not correct the information, and nobody would apologise.

8 For questions 9–16, read the text below. Use the word given in capitals at the end of each line to form a word that fits in the gap in the same line. There is an example at the beginning (0).

Pets care

One of the most surprising **(0)** ___*developments*___ in the treatment of patients in recent **DEVELOP**
years has been the use of pets. They are not just fun companions, but there is **(9)** _____ **PROVE**
that they can play an important therapeutic role in many cases. Doctors have reported that
patients have shown greater **(10)** _____ to fight their illness. Indeed, with the **DETERMINE**
aid of a pet, the road to **(11)** _____ is made much smoother. **RECOVER**

It has been found that young patients can easily build up a **(12)** _____ with a dog, cat **FRIEND**
or rabbit. This makes them feel less **(13)** _____ during their stay in hospital. Once a **MISERY**
week, a group of **(14)** _____ staff take the pets to see the patients who learn how to **VOLUNTEER**
feed them and handle them **(15)** _____ . **CARE**

As a result of several experimental programmes, it is now common **(16)** _____ that pets **KNOW**
reduce stress. However, it is important that, once such a programme has started, it must be
carried through to its conclusion.

If not, in some cases patients begin to become ill again.

Grammar

9 For questions 1–10 choose the word or phrase that best completes the sentence.

1 __ you make some tea, please?
   A Could
   B Did
   C Are
   D May

2 Oh! You __ bought me flowers!
   A can't have
   B mustn't have
   C couldn't have
   D shouldn't have

3 'Why were his eyes so red?'
   'He __ for eight hours.'
   A had studied
   B had been studying
   C has studied
   D is studying

4 Everyone loves Julia, __ ?
   A aren't they
   B doesn't she
   C don't they
   D isn't she

5 I think Tom has hurt __ .
   A him
   B he
   C his
   D himself

6 Did __ answer when you called?
   A anything
   B anybody
   C somewhere
   D everything

7 'Did you know where he was?'
   'No, I __ him since the day before.'
   A hadn't seen
   B haven't seen
   C hadn't been seeing
   D haven't been seeing

8 She __ go to the meeting, but she's still going.
   A mustn't
   B can't
   C doesn't have to
   D couldn't

9 He __ tired. He went to bed early.
   A should have been
   B must have been
   C can have been
   D needn't have been

10 Be careful, __ ?
   A aren't you
   B won't you
   C don't you
   D do you

Vocabulary

10 For questions 11–20 choose the word or phrase that best completes the sentence.

11 According __ my app, we'll be there at 5.40.
   A at
   B from
   C of
   D to

12 I hope you __ a success of your new career.
   A do
   B make
   C have
   D get

13 Let's take advantage __ the good weather.
   A of
   B on
   C off
   D in

14 If you practise, it will build your __ .
   A advice
   B business
   C confidence
   D difference

15 I got a job in a holiday camp, to __ some experience of working with children.
   A make
   B gain
   C give
   D take

16 I was going to go, but the weather put me __ .
   A out
   B over
   C up
   D off

17 Many species will __ out if global warming continues at this rate.
   A go
   B die
   C live
   D exit

18 This cup dates __ to the 13th century.
   A back
   B down
   C out
   D around

19 Do you have any __ that Mark stole it?
   A knowledge
   B experiment
   C analysis
   D proof

20 I'm so bored by this book. It's too __ .
   A repeating
   B similar
   C repetitive
   D same

Awareness

1 Which of these sentences are correct (C) and incorrect (I)?

1 It's not worth to fight about this. ___
2 I persuaded her going to the café with me. ___
3 She was happy to hear that you're coming. ___
4 Please don't make me do it all again. ___
5 Were you expecting finish by five o'clock? ___

6 You're not allowed talking during the show. ___
7 He doesn't remember to see her before. ___
8 Imagine standing by the edge of a volcano! ___
9 It wasn't cold enough to snow on the first day. ___
10 I hope seeing you soon. ___

How many did you get right? ☐

Grammar

-ing form

The -ing form is a verb with an -ing ending. We can use -ing forms:

- as nouns.
Reading in bed is very relaxing.

- after prepositions.
I'm thinking about volunteering.

- after the verb go when we talk about activities.
Ellen goes skiing every winter.

We also use the -ing form after certain verbs and phrases.

admit	fancy	it's no good	practise
avoid	feel like	it's no use	prefer
be used to	finish	it's (not) worth	prevent
can't help	forgive	keep	regret
can't stand	hate	like	risk
deny	have difficulty	love	spend time
dislike	imagine	(don't) mind	suggest
enjoy	involve	miss	worth

*I don't **feel like going** to the beach today.*
*It's **worth booking** tickets a long time before you plan to travel.*

to + infinitive

We use to + infinitive:

- to explain purpose.
*I went to the sports shop **to buy** some trainers.*

- after adjectives such as *afraid, scared, happy, glad, pleased, sad*, etc.
*I'm **sad to say** the weather is going to get worse.*

- after too + adjective or adjective + enough.
*The sea is **too cold to swim** in.*
*The sea isn't **warm enough to swim** in.*

We also use to + infinitive after certain verbs and phrases.

afford	arrange	expect	invite	offer	pretend	want
agree	ask	fail	learn	persuade	promise	would like
allow	choose	forget	manage	plan	refuse	
appear	decide	hope	need	prepare	seem	

*Maria **offered to help** the aid workers deliver supplies.*
***Would you like to come** camping with us?*

Infinitives without *to*

We use infinitives (without *to*) after:
- modal verbs.

You **must try** this.

- *had better* to give advice.

You **had better go** and see the doctor.

- *would rather* to talk about preference. We often use the word *than*.

She **would rather climb** a mountain than lie on a beach.

> ### Note
>
> 1 We use *let* + object + infinitive without *to* when we want to say that we give permission for someone to do something. It is only used in the active voice. In the passive we can use the verb *be allowed to*.
> The head teacher **let us go** home early.
> We **were allowed to go** home early.
>
> 2 We use *make* + object + infinitive without *to* when we want to say that we force a person to do something in the active voice, but in the passive we use *to* + infinitive.
> My dad **made me wash** his car again.
> I **was made to wash** Dad's car again.

-ing form or infinitive?

Some verbs can be followed by an *-ing* form or *to* + infinitive with no change in meaning. Some common verbs are *begin, bother, continue, hate, like, love* and *start*.
The aid workers **began to look / looking** for survivors.
I **loved to go / going** camping when I was younger.
We didn't **bother to have / having** a shower all weekend.

There are other verbs that can be followed by an *-ing* form or *to* + infinitive, but the meaning changes. Some common verbs are *go on, forget, regret, remember, stop* and *try*.
I **forgot buying** water. (I didn't remember that I had bought water.)
I **forgot to buy** water. (I didn't remember to buy water, so I don't have any.)

We **went on walking**. (They continued to walk.)
We **went on to walk** to the border. (They had been walking for a while, then continued walking to the border.)

I **regret not going** on the trip. (I didn't go on the trip, and now I regret it.)
We **regret to inform** you that tickets are now sold out. (We're sorry that we have to tell you this.)

He **remembers having** his passport at the airport. (He had his passport at the airport and now he remembers.)
He **remembered to apply** for a new passport. (He remembered first and then he applied for a passport.)

They **stopped driving** because they were tired. (They didn't drive anymore.)
They **stopped to have** a snack. (They stopped doing something so they could have a snack.)

Try turning it off and on again. (Do it, and see if that works.)
I **tried to** turn it on, but it didn't work. (I made the effort, but didn't succeed.)

13

Grammar exercises

2 **Choose the correct option to complete the sentences.**

1 You were very lucky *to survive* / *surviving* that earthquake!
2 I wouldn't risk *to go* / *going* out in this weather.
3 The power of nature never fails *amaze* / *to amaze* me.
4 Why did you refuse *to help* / *helping* him?
5 The performers went on *to play* / *playing* through the rain.
6 Do you think we'll be allowed *to visit* / *visiting* the site of the tornado?
7 Why don't you try *to look* / *looking* on the app for the information?
8 We weren't able to avoid *fall* / *falling* ill on our trip to India.
9 Did you manage *to get* / *get* in contact with your friend?
10 It's no use *to cry* / *crying* – that won't help!

3 **Use the prompts to write sentences with the -*ing* form or infinitive (with or without *to*).**

1 I / not / interested / make / lots of money

_____

2 we / not / afford / go / on holiday

_____

3 I / rather / play / chess / than / a computer game

_____

4 she / regret / not / study / harder / when she was at school

_____

5 Dan / stop / do / gymnastics / when he was twelve

_____

6 dive / off cliffs / is a dangerous hobby

_____

7 it / be / kind of you / help / us

_____

8 you / not / need / win every race

_____

4 **Complete the interview with the -*ing* form or infinitive (with or without *to*) of the verbs.**

Interviewer: When did you decide [1] _____ (become) a computer game creator?

Isabel: I don't really know. I've always enjoyed [2] _____ (play) games, but I don't remember [3] _____ (think) 'That's what I want [4] _____ (do) as a job when I'm older.' It just happened.

Interviewer: Was it difficult [5] _____ (get) started in the industry?

Isabel: Not for me. I learned [6] _____ (program) a computer when I was eight and I had spent a lot of time [7] _____ (create) things. So when I saw the job advertised, I expected [8] _____ (get) it. I was very confident!

Isabel: Would you like [9] _____ (give) some advice to young people who want [10] _____ (work) in the gaming industry?

Donna: You have to [11] _____ (love) computers and be good at [12] _____ (program). Keep [13] _____ (study), and don't give up [14] _____ (try). It's a great job.

5 Complete the sentences with the -*ing* form or infinitive (with or without *to*) of the verbs.

1 Do you remember _____ (meet) Tom last year?

2 I really regret _____ (not / go) to my cousin's wedding.

3 I regret _____ (inform) you that the train has been delayed by 30 minutes.

4 We stopped _____ (get) some lunch before continuing on our journey.

5 It's time you stopped _____ (be) so lazy.

6 After I had read her first book, I went on _____ (read) all of her others.

6 Correct the sentences where necessary. Tick those which do not need correcting.

1 I would rather to listen to the news.

_____

2 Try find out what went wrong.

_____

3 We were invited to join the group.

_____

4 It's not worth to spend so much time on this.

_____

5 The driver wouldn't let any more passengers to get on the bus.

_____

6 The hospital continued to admit new patients throughout the day.

_____

7 Complete the sentences with the correct form of *make* or *let*.

1 My mum won't _____ me come out because I have too much homework to do.

2 We were _____ to stay behind after school as a punishment.

3 If you don't want to do it, I won't _____ you. It's your choice.

4 Should we _____ the children stay up late? They want to watch the football match on TV.

5 Were you _____ to do lots of sports when you were at primary school?

6 Mum _____ me have a shower as soon as I got back from camping. I hadn't showered for days!

Vocabulary

Collocations and expressions

8 Match the beginnings (1–8) with the words (a–h) to form expressions.

1 the calm before the ☐	a	gathering
2 be down to ☐	b	clouds
3 be in hot ☐	c	storm
4 have your head in the ☐	d	water
5 get wind of ☐	e	check
6 steal someone's ☐	f	something
7 there are storm clouds ☐	g	earth
8 take a rain ☐	h	thunder

9 Complete the sentences with the expressions from Exercise 8.

1 If you get the attention or success that someone else was expecting, you _____ .

2 If a person is described as being _____ , they're sensible and practical.

3 When you're in the _____ , you know that things are going to get busy or difficult.

4 If you _____ , you find out about something secret or private.

5 If you're in _____, you're in big trouble.

6 When you need to move something to a later date, you have to _____ .

7 If you say there are _____ , you're expecting a difficult situation to develop.

8 A person with their _____ is not thinking realistically.

Exam practice

Sentence transformation

10 **Complete the second sentence so that it has a similar meaning to the first sentence, using the word given. Do not change the word given. You must use between two and five words.**

1 Mark's parents won't allow him to go camping before his exams.

Mark's parents _____ camping before his exams.   **LET**

2 I don't want to go training tonight.

I _____ training tonight.   **FEEL**

3 'Wash your hands before you eat.' Dad said.

Dad told me _____ my hands before I eat.   **FORGET**

4 They'd go diving, but they don't have enough money.

They _____ diving.   **AFFORD**

5 They forced us to run around the track three times.

We _____ around the track three times.   **MADE**

6 I need to work tonight. Can we go to the cinema another time?

I need to work tonight. Can we _____ on the cinema?   **RAIN**

7 I'm really sorry that I didn't try to help her.

I really _____ to help her.   **REGRET**

8 I always enjoy working with Emma. She's very practical and sensible.

I always enjoy working with Emma. She's very _____ .   **EARTH**

Open cloze

11 **Read the sentences and think of a word which best fits each gap. Use only one word in each gap.**

1 It's _____ use asking her. She won't help.

2 I'm not _____ to sleeping in such a small bed.

3 He'd rather miss lunch _____ leave the meeting early.

4 Why are you pretending _____ enjoy yourself?

5 I regret _____ volunteering to help deliver food parcels.

6 At school, we _____ made to wear uniform every day.

7 It's _____ remembering that the weather can change any minute.

8 I'd like to _____ some time exploring the local area.

Writing

12 **Write a paragraph about yourself in your notebook. Use these words.**

be afraid of   be good / terrible at   can't stand   enjoy   spend time   would rather ... than ...

Unit 14

1 Which of these sentences are correct (C) and incorrect (I)?

1 Today's earthquake was stronger last week's. ___
2 That's the bigest volcano I've ever seen. ___
3 Whales aren't as dangerous as sharks. ___
4 The sooner you finish the best it will be. ___
5 What's the most polluted city in the world? ___
6 We don't have time enough for this. ___
7 It was such a violent storm. ___
8 Dad explained it more clearly than a teacher. ___
9 5 a.m. is the earlyest I have ever got up. ___
10 It's too hot to go outside! ___

How many did you get right? ☐

Grammar

Comparison of adjectives and adverbs

We use the comparative to compare two people or things. We usually form the comparative by adding -er to an adjective or adverb. If the adjective or adverb has two or more syllables, we use the word *more*. We often use the word *than* after the comparative.
*Lake Baikal is **deeper than** the Caspian Sea.*
*Today's storm was over **more quickly than** yesterday's.*

We use the superlative to compare one person or thing with other people or things of the same type. We usually form the superlative by adding -est to the adjective or adverb. If the adjective or adverb has two or more syllables, we use the word *most*. We use the word *the* before the superlative.
*What is **the highest** volcano in the world?*
*Julia climbed **the most skilfully**.*

Spelling: hot → hot**ter** / hot**test** , brave → brav**er** / brav**est** , tiny → tin**ier** / tin**iest**

Some adjectives and adverbs are irregular and form their comparative and superlative in different ways.

Adjective / Adverb	Comparative	Superlative
good / well	better	the best
bad / badly	worse	the worst
many / more	more	the most
much	more	the most
little	less	the least
far	farther / further	the farthest / furthest

> **Note**
>
> 1 Some words like *hard*, *late*, *straight* and *fast* are both adjectives and adverbs.
> 2 Other words like *friendly*, *lovely*, *silly*, and *ugly* are not adverbs but adjectives, even though they end in -ly.
> 3 The words *hardly* (= barely) and *lately* (= recently) are not the adverbs of *hard* and *late*.

Other comparative structures

We use *as* + adjective / adverb + *as* to show that two people or things are similar in some way.
*Do you think the USA is **as big as** China?*

We use *not as / so* + adjective / adverb + *as* to show that one person or thing has less of a quality than another.
*This earthquake wasn't **as dangerous as** the last one.*

We use two clauses with *the* + comparative to show how one change causes another.
***The colder** the weather, **the higher** the risk of ice.*

too, enough, so and such

We use *too* + adjective / adverb to show that something is more than we want or need.
*It's **too far** to walk.*
*He was running **too quickly** for me to catch him.*

We use *(not)* adjective / adverb + *enough*, or *(not) enough* + noun to show that something is or isn't as much as we want or need.
*The water **isn't hot enough**.*
*We have **enough wood** to make a fire.*

We use *so* and *such* for emphasis. They are stronger than *very*.

• We use *so* + adjective / adverb.
*The rain was **so heavy**!*

• We use *such a* + (adjective) + noun.
*She is such **a brave explorer**.*

Note

We can also use *so* and *such* to emphasise characteristics that lead to a certain result or action.
*It was **such an uncomfortable journey that** I didn't sleep.*
*The wind was **so strong that** our tent blew away!*

Grammar exercises

2 **Choose the correct option to complete the sentences.**

1 She's the *most nice / nicest person* I've ever met.
2 We didn't get there as *quick / quickly* as we wanted to.
3 The *warm / warmer* the water, the more pleasant the swim.
4 You can't play as *good / well* as I do.
5 That was the *worse / worst* song I've ever heard.
6 Do you know the name of the *higher / highest* mountain in the world?
7 Cats are *more clever / cleverer* than dogs.
8 Storms happen more *frequently / frequent* in the summer.

3 **Complete the conversations with the comparative or superlative form of the adjectives.**
A
Tom: What's your favourite subject? I think maths is ¹ _____ (good).

Lucy: Are you serious? Maths is ² _____ (bad) subject in school. Even geography is
³ _____ (interesting) than maths – and I think geography is boring!

Tom: So, what do you like?

Lucy: For me, history is ⁴ _____ (interesting) subject.

B

Laura: Wow. That was ⁵ _____ (funny) film I've ever seen!

Jake: Do you think so? I think the first one was ⁶ _____ (funny) than that one.

Laura: I haven't seen the first one yet.

Jake: You'll love it. I've never laughed ⁷ _____ (loud) in my life!

Laura: Was it ⁸ _____ (exciting) than the second one as well?

Jake: Yes, it was definitely ⁹ _____ (entertaining) than the one we've just seen and a much
¹⁰ _____ (good) film in every way. You have to see it!

4 Rewrite the sentences with *(not) as ... as.*

1 The red bike is cheaper than the blue one.
The blue bike isn't _____ .

2 Earthquakes are scarier than thunderstorms.
Thunderstorms aren't _____ .

3 Paris and London are equally polluted.
London is _____ .

4 Donna speaks more clearly than Carla.
Carla doesn't _____ .

5 You and I play the guitar equally well.
I play the guitar _____ .

6 He drives much faster than she does.
She doesn't _____ .

7 My mum is taller than my dad.
My dad isn't _____ .

8 My brother and my sister are equally clever.
My sister is _____ .

5 Rewrite the sentences with *the* + comparative, *the* + comparative.

1 As it got darker, it got colder.
The *darker it got, the colder it got* _____ .

2 You will live longer if you are healthy.
The _____ .

3 As the man got closer, we became more nervous.
The closer _____ .

4 If you study harder, you will know more.
The harder _____ .

5 As he gets older, his hair gets greyer.
The _____ .

6 If they play their music loudly, the neighbours will get angry.
The louder _____ .

7 As the weather becomes warmer, people are happier.
The _____ .

8 As I work hard, I get tired.
The _____ .

6 Complete the sentences with *too* or *enough*.

1 This coffee isn't hot _____ .

2 This tea is _____ cold.

3 He's tall _____ to reach the shelf.

4 It's much _____ hot to sit in the garden.

5 Are you old _____ to drive?

6 No, I'm _____ young to drive.

7 We were _____ afraid to go outside.

8 There wasn't _____ time to finish our meal.

9 Don't get home _____ late tonight.

10 We'll catch the first bus if we get up early _____ .

7 Complete the sentences with *so* or *such*.

1 That was _____ an amazing film.

2 It was _____ a small earthquake that hardly anyone noticed it.

3 He talks _____ quickly that no one can understand him.

4 The storm began _____ suddenly that we all got wet.

5 It's _____ a beautiful day!

6 Your house is _____ lovely.

7 My uncle tells _____ boring stories.

8 I've never seen _____ a tiny computer.

Vocabulary

Prepositions

8 Complete the phrases with these prepositions. Use each preposition at least once.

by   from   on

1 be different _____

2 be surprised _____

3 do research _____

4 drop _____

5 hold something _____

6 live _____

7 prevent something / someone _____

8 recover _____

9 Complete the sentences with the correct form of the phrases from Exercise 8.

1 I don't know why I'm so _____ my brother. We're nearly the same age.

2 We _____ the dog _____ its collar until the owner arrived.

3 The fence is to _____ animals _____ leaving the field.

4 Have you done much _____ climate change?

5 I can't wait to climb again after I _____ this knee injury.

6 The price of houses has _____ 10% in the last year.

7 We were _____ the eruption of the volcano – no one was expecting it.

8 Giant pandas _____ the leaves and other parts of the bamboo plant.

Exam practice

Sentence transformation

10 Complete the second sentence so that it has a similar meaning to the first sentence, using the word given. Do not change the word given. You must use between two and five words.

1 Tanya and Sylvia are the same age.
Sylvia _____ Tanya. **OLD**

2 You can't play for the team because you're too slow at running.
You can't play for the team because you _____ at running. **FAST**

3 No one in the school dances better than Marco.
Marco _____ in the school. **THE**

4 The storm was so violent that our windows were broken.
It was _____ that our windows were broken. **SUCH**

5 I thought the test would be harder.
The test _____ I expected. **HARD**

6 Our hands and feet hurt because of the cold.
It _____ that our hands and feet hurt. **SO**

7 As our cat gets older, it becomes fatter.
The older our cat gets, _____ becomes. **THE**

8 We are too unfit to go skiing this year.
We are _____ skiing this year. **FIT**

Word formation

11 Use the word in capitals to form a word that fits in the gap.

1 It was the most _____ earthquake the country had ever suffered. **DESTROY**
2 Before the _____ , the village was evacuated. **ERUPT**
3 A _____ event was responsible for the extinction of the dinosaurs. **CATASTROPHE**
4 A _____ tsunami destroyed half the town. **MASS**
5 The avalanche was huge and, _____ , there were no survivors . **FORTUNATE**
6 The minotaur is a _____ beast. **MYTH**
7 The second eruption was much greater in _____ than the first. **INTENSE**
8 We had been vaccinated, and so were _____ to the disease. **RESIST**

Writing

12 Read the writing task and write your answer in 140–190 words in an appropriate style.

You see an announcement in an English-language magazine for young people. They are looking for adventure stories. Write a story beginning with this sentence:

When Alex woke up, it felt like a normal day – but then he remembered.

Your story must include:

• an unusual place
• an exciting event.

Awareness

1 **Which of these sentences are correct (C) and incorrect (I)?**

1 The paintings were did with a computer. ___
2 The film will be being produced next year. ___
3 Are you being interviewed at lunchtime? ___
4 We were showed the advert by the director. ___
5 Your laptop will be repaired tomorrow. ___

6 What has been done about the blog post? ___
7 The news were broadcast at 9 p.m. ___
8 They'll be being given some more homework. ___
9 This app is been used all over the world. ___
10 All the podcasts will have been uploaded by the end of the month. ___

How many did you get right? ☐

Grammar

The passive

We use the passive when:

- the action is more important than the person or thing that did the action (the agent).

*The article **was read** by thousands of people.*

- we don't know the agent, or it is not important.

*The film **will be released** in cinemas next month.*

> **Note**
>
> When it is important to mention the agent in a passive sentence, we use the word *by*. When we want to mention a tool or material in the passive sentence, we use the word *with*.
>
> *I was interviewed **by** a journalist.*
> *The photos were taken **with** a phone.*

The passive is formed with the verb *be* and a past participle. Notice how the active verb forms change to passive verb forms.

Tense	Active	Passive
present simple	take / takes	am / are / is taken
present continuous	am /are / is taking	am / are / is being taken
past simple	took	was / were taken
past continuous	was / were taking	was / were being taken
present perfect	have / has taken	have / has been taken
past perfect simple	had taken	had been taken
future simple	will take	will be taken
future perfect simple	will have taken	will have been taken

> **Note**
>
> There is no passive form for the future continuous, present perfect continuous or past perfect continuous.

We change an active sentence into a passive sentence in the following way:

- The object of the verb in the active sentence becomes the subject of the verb in the passive sentence.
- We use the verb *be* in the same tense as the main verb of the active sentence, together with the past participle of the main verb in the active sentence.

*They **were filming** her. → She **was being filmed**.*

In this example we do not know who was filming her and it is not very important, so we do not include this information in the passive sentence.

> **Note**
>
> After some verbs there are two objects, for example, *give*, *lend*, *send* and *show*. When we want to change an active sentence with two objects into the passive voice, one becomes the subject of the passive sentence and the other one remains an object. Which object we choose depends on what we want to emphasise. The structure is:
>
> subject [indirect object] + passive verb + direct object (+ *by* + agent).
> *He was shown* **the script** *(by the director).*
> OR
> subject [direct object] + passive verb + indirect object (+ *by* + agent).
> When a direct object is followed by an indirect object, we have to use a preposition (*to*, *for*, etc.) in front of the indirect object.
> **The script** *was shown* **to him** *(by the director).*

Grammar exercises

2 **Choose the correct option to complete the sentences.**

1 The show is *been / being* recorded at the moment.
2 My novel has been *made / making* into a film.
3 Your essay was *handed / handing* in late.
4 You'll *given / be given* a prize if you win.
5 Where was this photo *taken / took*?
6 Her books have been *read / reading* by millions of people.
7 You can't do that! It *isn't / doesn't* allowed.
8 The photos were *been / being* uploaded last night.
9 Where *are / is* most computer games produced?
10 Have you been *taught / teaching* how to use this camera?

3 **Write the sentences in the passive.**

1 They make films.
  Films _____.

2 They are making a film.
  A film _____.

3 They made a film.
  _____.

4 They were making a film.
  _____.

5 They have made a film.
  _____.

6 They had made a film.
  _____.

7 They will make a film.
  _____.

8 They are going to make a film.
  _____.

9 They will have made a film.
  _____.

4 Complete the sentences with the passive form of the verbs. Use the tense given.

1 This search engine _____ is used _____ (use) by more people than any other. *present simple passive*

2 The documentary _____ (watch) by over a million people. *past simple passive*

3 The politician _____ (interview) outside the town hall. *past continuous passive*

4 The next podcast _____ (not / upload) yet. *present perfect passive*

5 The attachments _____ (send) in a separate email. *future simple passive.*

6 When I checked my phone, fifteen voicemails _____ (leave). *past perfect passive*

7 The new homepage _____ (design) at the moment. *present continuous passive*

8 My online profile _____ (update) by the end of the week. *future perfect passive.*

5 Rewrite the sentences in the passive.

1 Someone had broken the TV.

_____

2 Simon will interview the actor.

_____

3 They have found a cure for the disease.

_____

4 They close the café at 5 p.m.

_____

5 A million people watched the documentary.

_____

6 They will have found him by now.

_____

7 They were making a lot of noise.

_____

8 A person is reviewing the film.

_____

6 Use the prompts to write sentences in the passive.

1 cheese / produce / in the UK

_____ .

2 the 2020 Olympics / hold / in Tokyo

_____ .

3 humans / send to Mars / by 2030

_____ .

4 *The Hunger Games* / write / by Suzanne Collins

_____ .

5 coffee / grow / in Italy

_____ .

6 Where / Mercedes cars / make

_____ .

7 When / your phone / steal

_____ .

8 the website / update / at the moment

_____ .

7 Complete the sentences with the correct active or passive form of the verbs.

1 My dad _____ (take) that photo of me, and it _____ (frame) by my uncle.

2 **A:** '_____ my jacket _____ (repair) yet?'

B: 'Yes, we _____ (mend) it this morning.'

3 I'm sure the competition _____ (win) by a South American team next year.

4 **A:** 'She _____ (write) her blog at the moment, so she can't talk to you.'

B: '_____ (you / ask) her to phone me, please?'

5 **A:** 'This video _____ (download) half a million times so far this year.'

B: 'I _____ (not / see) it yet.'

6 Last night we _____ (make) some pizzas, and they _____ (eat) very quickly.

Vocabulary

Phrasal verbs

8 Match the phrasal verbs (1–10) with their meanings (a–j).

1 bring over ☐	a	visit someone
2 bring up ☐	b	talk to someone you haven't seen for a while and find out their news
3 call back ☐	c	think carefully about something in order to make a decision
4 call in ☐	d	end a phone call
5 catch on ☐	e	take someone or something to a place
6 catch up ☐	f	return a phone call
7 hang on ☐	g	become popular or fashionable
8 hang up ☐	h	start discussing a subject
9 look at ☐	i	search for information
10 look up ☐	j	wait or be patient

9 Complete the sentences with the correct form of the phrasal verbs from Exercise 8.

1 Emily's having lunch at the moment. Could you _____ in fifteen minutes?

2 This app isn't very easy to use, so I don't think it will _____ .

3 I could _____ my spare laptop for you this afternoon.

4 I didn't want to leave a message, so I just _____ when you didn't answer.

5 Can we _____ booking a trip to Edinburgh?

6 Tom didn't know what the word meant, so he _____ it _____ in a dictionary.

7 It was great to _____ with Sarah yesterday and hear all her news.

8 My friends _____ to see me when I was ill.

9 The teacher _____ the issue of late homework.

10 If you _____ a moment, I'll see if Dr Green is available.

Exam practice

Sentence transformation

10 Complete the second sentence so that it has a similar meaning to the first sentence, using the word given. Do not change the word given. You must use between two and five words.

1 They weren't giving the children any attention.

The children _____ any attention.   **GIVEN**

2 They'll clean the house this afternoon.

The house _____ this afternoon.   **WILL**

3 Did your mum make this cake?

Was _____ your mum?   **BY**

4 Sam plays a very important role in this production.

A very important role _____ in this production.   **PLAYED**

5 By this time next year, they will have built a new sports centre in town.

By this time next year, a new sports centre _____ in town.   **BUILT**

6 I told you not to do that.

You _____ that.   **WERE**

7 I promised my mum I would return her call in half an hour.

I promised my mum _____ in half an hour.   **BACK**

8 It's an interesting idea, but I don't know if it will become popular.

It's an interesting idea, but I don't know if _____ .   **CATCH**

Multiple-choice cloze

11 For questions 1–8, decide which answer (A, B, C or D) best fits each gap.

1 How many of these ___ made every year?

A are   B be   C do   D done

2 My shirt was designed ___ a famous designer.

A with   B on   C by   D on

3 Gina was ___ interviewed by a TV reporter.

A in   B be   C doing   D being

4 How many calls have ___ made to the helpline?

A be   B been   C being   D were

5 I didn't know what 'host' meant, so I ___ it up in a dictionary.

A brought   B hung   C thought   D looked

6 By this time tomorrow, the new camera will ___ arrived.

A have   B had   C be   D been

7 I'm really looking forward to catching ___ with you at the weekend.

A in   B out   C up   D over

8 When we arrived, we ___ shown to our rooms by the manager.

A are   B were   C was   D did

Writing

12 Write six quiz questions in the passive in your notebook. Ask the class your questions. How many did your class get right?

Who were the Star Wars films directed by?

Unit 16

Awareness

1 **Which of these sentences are correct (C) and incorrect (I)?**

1 He is say to be the best singer in the school. ___
2 This must be finished by tomorrow. ___
3 The new sports centre is expected to be fantastic. ___
4 It is expect that the plane will arrive on time. ___
5 This city is considered being the safest in the world. ___
6 Marco is supposed to be a great tennis player. ___
7 It is understood that the government will make big changes. ___
8 That newspaper knows to be inaccurate. ___
9 This room needs be cleaned. ___
10 It is considered rude to leave the table without permission. ___

How many did you get right? ☐

Grammar

The passive: *-ing* form, infinitives and modal verbs

	Active	Passive
-ing form	taking	being taken
infinitive	take	be taken
infinitive + *to*	to take	to be taken
modal	can take	can be taken

*No one **likes being told** what to do.*
*He **agreed to be photographed**.*
*The filming **had better be finished** before dark.*
*All scripts **must be checked** carefully before they are given to the actors.*

The passive: impersonal and personal structures

We often use verbs like *believe, consider, know, expect, say, suppose, think* and *understand* in the passive voice. They can be used in an impersonal or a personal passive structure.
We form the impersonal passive structure with *it* + passive verb + *that* + clause.
People expect that the blog will soon have a million followers.
***It is expected that** the blog will soon have a million followers.*

We form the personal structure with noun + passive verb + *to* + infinitive.
Many people say that the internet has changed the way we think.
***The internet is said to have changed** the way we think.*

16

Grammar exercises

2 Rewrite the sentences in the passive.

1 Spectators mustn't throw anything onto the stage.
Nothing _must be thrown onto the stage_ _____ .

2 You need to edit your essay more carefully.
Your essay _____ .

3 No one can do it.
It _____ .

4 Somebody might have stolen the bag.
The bag _____ .

5 They'd better fix this.
This _____ .

6 You should switch it off.
It _____ .

3 Use the prompts to write sentences.

1 said / this film / boring / is / to be
_____

2 that / chimpanzees / believed / can use language / it / is
_____

3 he / enjoy / interviewed / doesn't / being
_____

4 that / thought / is / radio / is becoming / less popular / it
_____

5 considered / his best / his latest book / to be / is
_____

6 invited / photographed / they / to be / were /
_____

4 Rewrite the sentences in the impersonal passive.

1 They know that she is responsible for the app's success.
It _is known that she is responsible for the app's success_ _____ .

2 They think that he is going to sell his business.
It _____ .

3 People believe that life exists on other planets.
It _____ .

4 They say that he works harder than anyone.
It _____ .

5 Some people believe that black cats are lucky.
It _____ .

6 They say that Katie is a great photographer.
It _____ .

7 People expect the film to be popular.

It _____ .

8 People understand that journalists travel a lot .

It _____ .

5 Rewrite the sentences from Exercise 4 in the personal passive.

1 _She is known to be responsible for the app's success_ _____ .

2 _____ .

3 _____ .

4 _____ .

5 _____ .

6 _____ .

7 _____ .

8 _____ .

6 Find one mistake in each sentence. Then correct the mistakes.

1 The computer ought be switched off.

_____

2 He is said that social media is damaging social relationships.

_____

3 I don't like be lied to.

_____

4 You'd better asking for permission before you post the photos.

_____

5 Documentaries is said to be educational.

_____

6 This TV drama is expecting to win lots of awards.

_____

7 Complete the sentences with one word in each gap.

1 _____ is thought that solar power is one solution to our energy problems.

2 This phone _____ considered to be the best on the market.

3 The ticket prices _____ be found on the website.

4 I would like my video _____ be watched by millions of people.

5 It is expected _____ the product will get great reviews.

6 Her fans enjoyed _____ given the chance to meet her.

7 Last year's plans _____ thought to be very ambitious.

8 Your work should _____ backed up every day.

16

Vocabulary

Word formation

8 Match the words (1–8) with their meanings (a–h).

1	act		**a**	find a way of dealing with a problem or difficult situation
2	danger		**b**	a magazine about a particular subject
3	engine		**c**	do something
4	journal		**d**	ideas about how to govern a country
5	nature		**e**	all the plants, animals and things that are not made by people
6	operate		**f**	the part of a machine that produces power
7	politics		**g**	use or control a machine or make it work
8	solve		**h**	the possibility of something bad happening

9 Use the word in capitals to form a word that fits in the gap.

1 Daniel is training to be a _____ .   JOURNAL

2 We can't record this news story without a sound _____ .   ENGINE

3 It's _____ to ride a bike in the city without a helmet.   DANGER

4 What skills do you need to be a camera _____ ?   OPERATE

5 I love films with plenty of _____ and special effects.   ACT

6 We need to work together to find a _____ to this problem.   SOLVE

7 My brother wants to be a _____ when he grows up.   POLITICS

8 There haven't been many _____ disasters in this area.   NATURE

Exam practice

Sentence transformation

10 Complete the second sentence so that it has a similar meaning to the first sentence, using the word given. Do not change the word given. You must use between two and five words.

1 They might build a new sports centre in town.
A new sports centre _____ in town.   **BUILT**

2 We have to write the headlines by 3 p.m.
The headlines _____ by 3 p.m.   **WRITTEN**

3 People know the moon is not made of cheese.
The moon _____ made of cheese.   **BE**

4 The actor thinks it's OK when people ask him for selfies.
The actor _____ for selfies.   **MIND**

5 They say she has millions of online followers .
It _____ she has millions of online followers.   **SAID**

6 People expect the podcast to win a prize.
The podcast _____ win a prize.   **EXPECTED**

7 They let us swim in the sea.
We _____ in the sea.   **ALLOWED**

8 They have just reported that the game is over.
It _____ that the game is over.   **BEEN**

Multiple-choice cloze

11 **For questions 1–8, decide which answer (A, B, C or D) best fits each gap.**

1 Julia is ___ to be an excellent dancer.
  A told   **B** said   **C** spoken   **D** heard

2 It is ___ good manners to say 'Thank you' after a meal.
  A known   **B** expected   **C** considered   **D** said

3 The journalist was delighted ___ be given the award.
  A to   **B** at   **C** have   **D** having

4 Some celebrities can't stand ___ photographed all the time.
  A it   **B** to   **C** be   **D** being

5 All accidents ___ be reported immediately.
  A are   **B** must   **C** need   **D** have

6 It ___ known that smoking is very bad for your health.
  A are   **B** has   **C** does   **D** is

7 Mark is ___ to be living in Spain now.
  A believed   **B** hoping   **C** knowing   **D** better

8 We were ___ to watch the programme being recorded.
  A let   **B** allowed   **C** could   **D** might

Writing

12 **Read the writing task and write your answer in 140–190 words in an appropriate style.**

You see an announcement on your college website asking for film reviews. Write a review of a film that you particularly like or dislike. Include information on the characters and plot, and a recommendation.

Grammar

1 **Complete the text with the *-ing* form or infinitive (with or without *to*) of the verbs.**

My name is Natasha. I'm 13 years old, and I want [1] _____ (be) an Olympic athlete. I enjoy [2] _____ (run) and [3] _____ (jump), but the event I would like [4] _____ (become) champion at is the javelin. I'm very lucky [5] _____ (have) a great coach My coach makes me [6] _____ (train) really hard every day, and expects me [7] _____ (do) my best all the time. We spend a lot of time [8] _____ (practise) after school and at weekends, too. Sometimes it's difficult [9] _____ (get) up early on Saturday and Sunday mornings. Often I feel like [10] _____ (stay) in bed all day, but it's no use [11] _____ (complain) because this is something that I've chosen [12] _____ (do). My coach refuses [13] _____ (let) me give up. I don't mind [14] _____ (do) what he tells me though – he is my dad!

2 **Complete the sentences with the comparative or superlative form of the adjectives.**

1 That was _____ (good) football match ever!

2 Geography is _____ (interesting) than maths.

3 That's _____ (bad) flood I've ever seen!

4 I don't want to walk _____ (far) than the bus stop.

5 Who has _____ (big) tent?

6 The typhoon was _____ (strong) than the hurricane.

7 That's _____ (ridiculous) thing I have ever heard.

8 A hippopotamus is _____ (dangerous) than an elephant.

3 **Rewrite the sentences in the passive.**

1 Someone needs to wash the car.
The car _____ .

2 People will never forget him.
He _____ .

3 They are catching a lot of fish.
A lot of fish _____ .

4 They teach computer science at this college.
Computer science _____ .

5 You have to feed the cat twice a day.
The cat _____ .

6 People should send their script ideas as an attachment.
Script ideas _____ .

7 Someone gave me directions.
I _____ .

8 No one said anything about the problem.
Nothing _____ .

4 **Rewrite the sentences in the passive in two ways.**

1 People think the firefighters responded quickly to the incident.

   a It _____ .

   b The firefighters _____ .

2 They say that computers have made life easier.

   a It _____ .

   b Computers _____ .

3 People believe that the new film is the director's best.

   a It _____ .

   b The new film _____ .

4 They know there is a risk of avalanches on the mountain.

   a It _____ .

   b There _____ .

5 **Choose the correct option to complete the sentences.**

1 It's hard to avoid *making / to make* mistakes.

2 She refused *saying / to say* anything about her private life.

3 What's the *better / best* film you've ever seen?

4 This chat room isn't as useful *as / like* the one I tried yesterday.

5 The TV studio was *equip / equipped* with the latest recording technology.

6 *It / He* is thought that the universe is 14 billion years old.

7 Why did he regret *to be / being* given the money?

8 Marko is said *to have / having* the best online profile.

6 **Find one mistake in each sentence. Then correct the mistakes.**

1 She is believed that working in television is very enjoyable.

_____

2 My phone was broke by my little brother.

_____

3 The quicker you run, the soonest you'll get there.

_____

4 This app is not as popular like that one.

_____

5 Oh no! I forgot switching off the printer.

_____

6 You had better to give that back to Tom.

_____

7 Nature documentaries are said being very expensive to make.

_____

8 That's the most funny joke I've ever heard.

_____

Exam practice

7 For questions 1–8, read the text below and think of a word which best fits each gap. Use only one word in each gap. There is an example at the beginning (0).

A young contender

(0) ___ , bowls is thought of as a game which is played by senior citizens, so the announcement that a ten year old will be taking **(1)** ___ in the National Bowls Championship has come as a shock to many players.

At the age of five, Ean Morton swapped his football boots for a set of bowls, which once **(2)** ___ to his great grandmother. He liked bowls at once, but it wasn't easy for Ean because he **(3)** ___ to play against people who could take **(4)** ___ of his inexperience. Although Ean did not **(5)** ___ a success of bowls instantly, he refused to allow it to spoil his enjoyment of it, and he continued to practise.

Now, Ean is more than a match for most of his opponents. He is very excited **(6)** ___ playing in the tournament, but admits that he doesn't really **(7)** ___ what to expect. His father, who will also be playing in the championship, is more optimistic. He believes that Ean will reach the top and is prepared to **(8)** ___ by him every step of the way.

0	A	Conservatively	(B)	Traditionally	C	Customarily	D	Practically
1	A	play	B	bit	C	piece	D	part
2	A	owned	B	belonged	C	possessed	D	effected
3	A	had	B	must	C	ought	D	would
4	A	benefit	B	gain	C	profit	D	advantage
5	A	be	B	do	C	have	D	make
6	A	for	B	from	C	about	D	with
7	A	know	B	realise	C	recognise	D	understand
8	A	support	B	set	C	stand	D	back

8 For questions 9–16, read the text below and think of a word which best fits each gap. Use only one word in each gap. There is an example at the beginning (0).

Bamboo

Bamboos are the **(0)** _fastest_ growing plants in the world. Even in countries like England, **(9)** _____ the plant does not grow naturally, it is known to be capable **(10)** _____ increasing in height by 15 centimetres in just 24 hours.

Such rapid growth is necessary because the plant has only 8–12 weeks before the dry weather comes to go from ground level to its maximum height, **(11)** _____ may be as much as 15 metres.

Bamboos are quite demanding. Not **(12)** _____ do they need a great deal of water to grow so quickly, but they also need deep soil **(13)** _____ that their roots can stay warm at colder times of the year. This means the gardener must make sure the ground is not **(14)** _____ stony for the plant to grow on.

Although bamboos used to be quite rare in British gardens, they have recently gained popularity with British gardeners. This is because they are green all the year round, **(15)** _____ are no insects in Britain which destroy them and they can grow so close together that not even a cat is thin **(16)** _____ to squeeze through.

Grammar

9 For questions 1–10, choose the word or phrase that best completes the sentence.

1 You promised ___ me to the cinema tonight!
A take
B taking
C to take
D taken

2 The teacher wouldn't let us ___ on time!
A leave
B leaving
C to leave
D left

3 I've been to ___ lessons than that.
A much interesting
B most interesting
C the most interesting
D more interesting

4 The nearer the time comes, ___ I get.
A more anxious
B the more anxious
C most anxious
D the most anxious

5 How many people is this search engine ___ ?
A used with
B using with
C used by
D using by

6 This medicine should only ___ to your dog.
A give
B be give
C given
D be given

7 Dan ___ the strongest candidate.
A is said to be
B is saying to be
C is said being
D says being

8 I can't let you in. You aren't ___ .
A too old
B old enough
C enough old
D too young

9 The film was ___ that I couldn't sleep that night.
A so scary
B scary so
C such scary
D such a scary

10 She didn't remember ___ her charger.
A to brought
B to bringing
C bringing
D to bring

Vocabulary

10 For questions 11–20, choose the word or phrase that best completes the sentence.

11 You'll get into ___ water if you're late for work again.
A cold
B blue
C hot
D rough

12 Dad brought ___ the issue of screen time.
A up
B out
C over
D round

13 We have done a lot of research ___ this subject.
A off
B of
C over
D on

14 Sally has got her ___ in the clouds.
A face
B head
C hair
D eyes

15 Can you call ___ on Grandad this afternoon?
A back
B in
C out
D up

16 She is very different ___ her sister.
A from
B against
C off
D compared

17 Let's ___ a rain check on that.
A get
B have
C make
D take

18 He didn't want to leave a message, so he hung ___ .
A in
B on
C out
D up

19 I hope Mum doesn't get ___ of the surprise!
A clouds
B earth
C wind
D water

20 I think this peace is the calm before the ___ .
A storm
B flood
C rain
D thunder

Awareness

1 Which of these sentences are correct (C) and incorrect (I)?

1 She said that she liked computers.   ___
2 My teacher told I to be quiet.   ___
3 He asked did I wanted to eat something.   ___
4 I told I had been working all day.   ___
5 What did he say you?   ___

6 She asked me when I had made my decision.   ___
7 They asked us if we liked football?   ___
8 You said that you weren't coming.   ___
9 He said me he was reading.   ___
10 Tom told me he would fix it.   ___

How many did you get right? ☐

Grammar

Reported speech: statements

When we report direct speech, we usually change the verb used by the speaker by putting it back one tense.

Direct speech	Reported speech
present simple	past simple
'He **enjoys** acting,' she said.	She said (that) he **enjoyed** acting.
present continuous	past continuous
'She **is studying** chemistry,' he said.	He said (that) she **was studying** chemistry.
present perfect simple	past perfect simple
'They **have passed** their exams,' she said.	She said (that) they **had passed** their exams.
present perfect continuous	past perfect continuous
'They **have been looking** for games,' she said.	She said (that) they **had been looking** for games.
past simple	past perfect simple
'She **went** for a job interview,' he said.	He said (that) she **had gone** for a job interview.
past continuous	past perfect continuous
'He **was listening** to music,' she said.	She said (that) he **had been listening** to music.

Other changes in verb forms are as follows:

can	could
'He **can** play the trumpet,' she said.	She said (that) he **could** play the trumpet.
may	might
'He **may** be late,' she said.	She said (that) he **might** be late.
must	had to
'He **must** get good grades to study law,' she said.	She said (that) he **had to** get good grades to study law.
will	would
'They **will** go to France,' she said.	She said (that) they **would** go to France.

> **Note**
>
> **1** We often use the verbs *say* and *tell* in reported speech. We follow *tell* with an object.
>   They **said** we should start our own business.
>   They **told** us we should start our own business.
> **2** We can leave out *that*.
>   He **said that** he preferred Spanish.
>   He **said** he preferred Spanish.
> **3** Remember to change pronouns and possessive adjectives where necessary.
>   '**We** are having a video call,' he said. → He said (that) **they** were having a video call.
>   'That's **my** laptop,' she said. → She said (that) that was **her** laptop.
> **4** The following tenses and words don't change in reported speech: past perfect simple, past perfect continuous, *would*, *could*, *might*, *should*, *ought to*, *used to*, *had better*, and *mustn't* and *must* when they refer to certainty (not necessity or obligation).

Reported speech: changes in time and place

When we report direct speech, there are often changes in words that show time and place too.

now	then
'I'm resting **now**,' she said.	She said she was resting **then**.
today	that day
'They're working from home **today**,' he said.	He said they were working from home **that day**.
tonight	that night
'I want to see a film **tonight**,' she said.	She said she wanted to see a film **that night**.
yesterday	the previous day / the day before
'I wasn't well **yesterday**,' he said.	He said he hadn't been well **the previous day** / **the day before**.
last week / month	the previous week / month /, the week / month before
'He left work **last month**,' she said.	She said he had left work **the previous month** / **the month before**.
tomorrow	the next day / the following day
'We'll finish the report **tomorrow**,' she said.	She said they would finish the report **the next day** / **the following day**.
next week / month	the following week / month
'I'm going on a course **next week**,' she said.	She said she was going on a course **the following week**.
this / these	that / those
'This is my desk,' she said.	She said that was her desk.
ago	before
'The meeting started an hour **ago**,' she said.	She said the meeting had started an hour **before**.
at the moment	at that moment
'He's working at the moment,' she said.	She said he was working at that moment.
here	there
'Your phone is **here**,' he said.	He said my phone was **there**.

Reported speech: questions

When we report questions, changes in tenses, pronouns, possessive adjectives, time and place are the same as in reported statements. In reported questions, the verb follows the subject as in ordinary statements and we do not use question marks.

When a direct question has a question word, we use this word in the reported question.
*'**When** did you decide to apply for the job?' he asked.*
*He asked **when** I had decided to apply for the job.*

When a direct question does not have a question word, we use *if* or *whether* in the reported question.
'Have you changed your password?' she asked.
*She asked **if / whether** I had changed my password.*

Grammar exercises

2 Choose the correct option to complete the sentences.

1 You didn't *say / tell* me you were ill.

2 My dad *said / told* there was a message for me.

3 Max *says / tells* some very funny stories.

4 Amelia *said / told* Ben how to log in to the system.

5 Who *said / told* you could do that?

6 Why didn't you *say / tell* it was your birthday?

7 I didn't *say / tell* anyone I was going on holiday.

8 His manager *said / told* that he had done a great job.

3 Complete the conversations using reported speech and the words given.

1 **A:** Grace has two brothers.
   B: But you said *(that) she had three*_____ . (three)

2 **A:** We're going to Aunt Jenny's house.
   B: But you said _____ . (Grandma's house)

3 **A:** Freddie has bought a new skateboard.
   B: But you said _____ . (a bike)

4 **A:** The kids have been sleeping.
   B: But they said _____ . (play)

5 **A:** I broke my mobile phone.
   B: But you said _____ . (laptop)

6 **A:** We were watching TV.
   B: But your mum said _____ . (listening to music)

7 **A:** Dan can only speak Italian and French.
   B: But he said _____ . (Chinese)

8 **A:** We'll go to the beach tomorrow.
   B: But you said _____ . (today)

4 Complete the reported sentences with the time and place.

1 'I don't like it here,' he said.
   He said he didn't like it _____ .

2 'We're going home today,' they said.
   They said they were going home _____ .

3 'I felt ill last night,' she said.
   She said she had felt ill _____ .

4 'I'll buy you a present tomorrow,' he told her.
   He told her he'd buy her a present _____ .

5 'This is great,' she said.
   She said _____ was great.

6 'I told Jake about it two weeks ago,' he said.
   He said he had told Jake about it _____ .

7 'I'm working at the moment,' she said.
   She said she was working _____ .

8 'Your bag is here on the chair,' he said to me.
   He told me my bag was _____ on the chair.

5 **Rewrite the sentences in reported speech.**

1 'I was really happy there,' he said.
   He said _____ .

2 'We love this building,' they said.
   They said _____ .

3 'I went to France last month,' she said.
   She said _____ .

4 'He'll have a party next week,' I said.
   I said _____ .

5 'She's giving a presentation at the moment,' he said.
   He said _____ .

6 'We are going out tonight,' they said.
   They said _____ .

7 'Yesterday was a beautiful day,' she said.
   She said _____ .

8 'I can't help you now,' he said to me.
   He said _____ .

6 **Complete the reported questions.**

1 'What time did you get up this morning?' she asked me.
   She asked me _____ .

2 'Do you have any money?' he asked her.
   He asked her _____ .

3 'What do you think about this film?' I asked him.
   I asked him _____ .

4 'Where is my computer?' she asked me.
   She asked me _____ .

5 'Are you having a meeting?' he asked them.
   He asked me _____ .

6 'Did you enjoy the conference?' she asked me.
   She asked him _____ .

7 Rewrite the conversation in reported speech.

1 **Matt:** 'How old are you?'

He asked her *how old she was* _____ .

2 **Eva:** 'I'm seventeen.'

She said _____ .

3 **Matt:** 'Can you sing?'

He asked her _____ .

4 **Eva:** 'I can sing very well.'

She said _____ .

5 **Matt:** 'What is your favourite kind of music?'

He asked her _____ .

6 **Eva:** 'I like hip-hop and jazz.'

She said _____ .

7 **Matt:** 'Do you want to join my band?'

He asked her _____ .

8 **Eva:** 'No, I don't want to.'

She said _____ .

Vocabulary

Collocations and expressions

8 Match 1–8 with a–h to form phrases.

1	get the	☐	**a**	job
2	hand in	☐	**b**	your notice
3	work in	☐	**c**	sack
4	a part-time	☐	**d**	a job offer
5	reject	☐	**e**	staff
6	retail	☐	**f**	experience
7	take on	☐	**g**	shifts
8	work	☐	**h**	management

9 Complete the sentences with the correct form of the phrases from Exercise 8.

1 When you _____ , you work either during the day or night.

2 If you _____ , you formally say that you are going to leave your job.

3 I want to work in a shop, to get some _____ .

4 Sophie should work _____ because she enjoys leading and organising.

5 If you _____ , you decide that it isn't important enough for you to accept.

6 When somebody _____ , they are told to leave their job.

7 He got _____ to earn some money while he was studying.

8 When a company _____ , it employs new workers.

Exam practice

Sentence transformation

10 Complete the second sentence so that it has a similar meaning to the first sentence, using the word given. Do not change the word given. You must use between two and five words.

1 'Have you done your homework?' my dad asked me.

My dad asked me _____ my homework.   **IF**

2 'We're going skiing next month,' she said.

She said they _____ month.   **FOLLOWING**

3 'We have to leave soon,' said John.

John said _____ soon.   **THEY**

4 'She may be lost,' I said.

I said that _____ lost.   **MIGHT**

5 'What time did you get home?' she asked me.

She asked me _____ got home.   **HAD**

6 'The boys are expecting a party tonight,' he said.

He said that _____ a party that night.   **WERE**

7 'Your book is here on the sofa,' she said to me.

She said that _____ on the sofa.   **THERE**

8 'Does she have any experience?' he asked me.

He asked me _____ any experience.   **WHETHER**

Word formation

11 Use the word in capitals to form a word that fits in the gap.

1 You need a _____ of skills to work here.   **COMBINE**

2 I'm thinking of doing some _____ work.   **VOLUNTEER**

3 He said that _____ , in that job, the more you worked, the more you   **BASIC**
got paid.

4 Are you _____ to do that job?   **QUALIFY**

5 Sara thinks being a doctor would be a very _____ job.   **REWARD**

6 Camera operators sometimes work in _____ conditions.   **CHALLENGE**

7 If you are _____ , you work for yourself.   **EMPLOY**

8 Zak is really _____ about art.   **PASSION**

Writing

12 Write six reported speech sentences in your notebook which are true for you. Here are some ideas:

- What was the first thing someone said to you today / yesterday?
- What was the first thing you said today / yesterday?
- What questions did you ask / were you asked yesterday?

Awareness

1 **Which of these sentences are correct (C) and incorrect (I)?**

1 I asked her help me. ___
2 She told him sitting down. ___
3 Did I remind you to reply to that email? ___
4 You promised to call me. ___
5 Why did he insist on stay so long? ___

6 I suggested going to bed early that night. ___
7 He asked me to not shout. ___
8 They refused leaving at the end of the show. ___
9 Did he accuse you of lying? ___
10 Our manager told us to go home early. ___

How many did you get right? ☐

Grammar

Reported speech: commands and requests

When we report commands, we usually use *tell* + object + *to* + infinitive.
'Be quiet!' he said.
He **told us to be** quiet.

'Send me the file this evening,' she said to her friend.
She **told her friend to send** her the file that evening.'

When we report a request, we usually use *ask* + object + *to* + infinitive.
'Can you help the customer, please?' he asked.
He **asked me to help** the customer.
(Also: *He asked if I could help the customer.*)

'Please don't stay late,' she said.
She **asked them not to stay** late.

Reporting verbs

Apart from the verbs *say*, *tell* and *ask*, we can also use other verbs to report what someone says more accurately. Notice the different structures.

verb + to + infinitive	
decide	'I think I'll come in early tomorrow,' he said. He **decided to come** in early the next day.
refuse	'I won't come in early,' she said. She **refused to come** in early.
offer	'Shall I help you?' she said. She **offered to help** me.
promise	'Don't worry, I'll help you,' he said. He **promised to help** me.
verb + object + to + infinitive	
advise	'If I were you, I'd apply for the job,' he said. He **advised me to** apply for the job.
remind	'Don't forget to apply for the job,' she said. She **reminded me to apply** for the job.

verb + *-ing* form	
deny	'I didn't see your password,' he said. He **denied seeing** my password.
suggest	'Let's change the password,' she said. She **suggested changing** the password.
verb + preposition + *-ing* form	
apologise for	'I'm sorry I was late for the meeting,' he said. He **apologised for being** late for the meeting.
insist on	'Don't be silly. I will print the documents for you,' she said. She **insisted on printing** the documents for me.
verb + object + preposition + *-ing* form	
accuse sb of	'I think you took my headphones,' he said. He **accused me of taking** his headphones.
congratulate sb on / for	'You won an award. Well done!' she said. She **congratulated me on winning** an award.

Grammar exercises

2 **Choose the correct option to complete the sentences.**

1 Simon refused *to help / helping* me.
2 You *promised / suggested* to buy me a new phone case.
3 Never apologise for *tell / telling* the truth.
4 My doctor *insisted / advised* me to get more sleep.
5 The head teacher congratulated Tom on *pass / passing* his exams.
6 He *denied / refused* stealing my calculator.
7 I accused her of *be / being* rude.
8 Sara didn't remind me *phone / to phone* her yesterday.
9 She *offered / advised* to pay for my ticket.
10 We decided *going / to go* to the conference.

3 **Complete the sentences using reported speech and the verbs.**

1 My dad congratulated me on _____ (get) the job.
2 Why did he decide _____ (move) to Italy?
3 Sophie advised her brother _____ (work) on his English verbs.
4 The children denied _____ (break) the tablet.
5 She apologised for _____ (call) so early in the morning.
6 He was accused of _____ (cheat) in the exam.
7 Dan offered _____ (check) my CV.
8 Did you remind her _____ (take) her suitcase?
9 I suggested _____ (contact) the local shop.
10 They refused _____ (increase) his salary.

4 Rewrite the sentences in reported speech with these verbs.

| accuse | apologise | congratulate | deny | remind | suggest |

1 'You're lying to me,' she said.

She _____ .

2 'Don't forget to bring some fresh water,' she said to him.

She _____ .

3 'I'm really sorry that I got angry,' I said to her.

I _____ .

4 'I didn't lose the document,' she said.

She _____ .

5 'Why don't we arrange a meeting?' he said.

He _____ .

6 'You finished the project. Well done!' she said to him.

She _____ .

5 Rewrite the commands and requests in reported speech.

1 'Don't touch that button!' she said to him.

_____

2 'Finish your dinner,' he said to me.

_____

3 'Please don't do that,' he said to her.

_____

4 'Don't forget to close the window,' she said to him.

_____

5 'Don't wait for me,' he said to her.

_____

6 'Please be careful,' she said to me.

_____

6 Find one mistake in each sentence. Then correct the mistakes.

1 He refused talking about his interview.

_____

2 She asked me work a little longer.

_____

3 They advised us investing in the company.

_____

4 You promised give me your old printer.

_____

5 He asked his mother to not wake him up early.

_____

6 Did you remember Amelia to check her bank balance?

_____

7 Rewrite the reported speech in direct speech.

1 Carla asked Ben what they should do. Ben suggested calling the helpline.

Carla: *What should we do?*

Ben: *Let's / Why don't we call the helpline.*

2 Sam accused Mark of stealing his book. Mark denied it.

Sam: _____

Mark: _____

3 Dan asked Maria if she wanted to go out or stay in. She decided to stay in.

Dan: _____

Maria: _____

4 Her manager told Anna to go home. But Anna refused.

Manager: _____

Anna: _____

5 Tom apologised for forgetting to buy milk. Eva reminded him the shop was open until 10 p.m.

Tom: _____

Eva: _____

6 Harry offered to buy Kate a sandwich. Kate insisted on buying her own.

Harry: _____

Kate: _____

7 Alex asked when they were going to the beach. Dad promised to take them the next day.

Alex: _____

Dad: _____

Vocabulary

Prepositions

8 Complete the phrases with these prepositions. Some prepositions can be used more than once.

| in | of | on | to |

1 find a solution _____

2 _____ my opinion

3 to be out _____ work

4 to be _____ debt

5 to react _____ something

6 _____ behalf of

7 reach the top _____

8 arrive / be _____ time

9 Complete the sentences with the correct form of the phrases from Exercise 8.

1 If you don't arrive at work _____ , you won't have a job for long.

2 It took a long time to _____ the problem, but we did it.

3 How did Simon _____ that difficult situation? Did he panic?

4 At the age of 50, Julia had finally _____ her chosen career.

5 _____ , that was a really silly decision.

6 If you have good skills, you won't _____ for very long.

7 _____ everyone here, I'd like to thank you for all your hard work.

8 Don't use credit cards if you don't want to _____ .

Exam practice

Sentence transformation

10 **Complete the second sentence so that it has a similar meaning to the first sentence, using the word given. Do not change the word given. You must use between two and five words**

1 'I'm sorry I'm late,' she said.
   She _____ late.   **APOLOGISED**

2 'No, I won't do what you say,' she said to him.
   She _____ said.   **REFUSED**

3 'Let's do a video call,' said John.
   John _____ a video call.   **DOING**

4 'You should go and see a doctor,' I said to her.
   I _____ and see a doctor.   **HER**

5 'I didn't make a mistake,' he said.
   He _____ a mistake.   **MAKING**

6 'Shall I make a cup of coffee?' he said.
   He _____ a cup of coffee.   **OFFERED**

7 I hope you can solve my problem.
   I hope you can _____ my problem.   **FIND**

8 At the moment, Greg hasn't got a job.
   Greg is _____ at the moment.   **OUT**

Open cloze

11 **Read the sentences and think of a word which best fits each gap. Use only one word in each gap.**

1 I'd like to thank you _____ behalf of everyone here.

2 She reminded me _____ send my CV.

3 It's the most interesting job in the world, _____ my opinion.

4 It took five days to reach the top _____ the mountain.

5 Congratulations _____ your recent success.

6 I apologised _____ missing the start of the meeting.

7 My boss asked me _____ I could work on Sunday.

8 'Don't forget to send that email,' she _____ to her secretary.

Writing

12 **Read the writing task and write your answer in 140–190 words in an appropriate style.**

Last summer, you worked in a children's activity camp. The organiser has asked you to write a report because some of the children said they hadn't enjoyed the activities. Write a report outlining what the problems were, and suggest some ways to improve the children's experience.

Awareness

1 Which of these sentences are correct (C) and incorrect (I)?

1 If you will travel first class, you will be more comfortable. ____

2 They won't let us in if we don't have tickets. ____

3 We'd stay in a hotel if it hadn't cost so much. ____

4 I wouldn't have known if she hadn't told me. ____

5 If you heat ice, it melts. ____

6 She'd come if you would ask her. ____

7 If you would have had lunch, you wouldn't be hungry now. ____

8 If I were you, I wouldn't do that. ____

9 Don't let him in the house if he calls round. ____

10 We'll show you the city if you would visit. ____

How many did you get right? ☐

Grammar

Zero conditional

If clause	Main clause
present simple	present simple

We use the zero conditional to talk about the results of an action or situation that are always true. We can use *when* instead of *if*.
If you **ride** a bike, you **don't pollute** the atmosphere.
When you **ride** a bike, you **don't pollute** the atmosphere.
You **don't pollute** the atmosphere *if* / *when* you **ride** a bike.

> **Note**
> If the conditional clause comes before the main clause, you need a comma.
> ***If you exercise regularly***, *you stay fit.*

First conditional

If clause	Main clause
present simple	*will* + infinitive (without *to*)

We use the first conditional to talk about the results of an action or situation that will probably happen now or in the future.
If we **have** *enough money, we***'ll go** *to Brazil.*
We **won't swim** *in the sea if* **isn't** *warm.*

We can use *can*, *could*, *may* or *might* in the main clause instead of *will*. We can also use an imperative.
If you don't like flying, you **can take** *a train.*
If you enjoy visiting art galleries, **go** *to Florence.*

We can use *unless* in conditional sentences. It means the same as *if not*.
We won't go to the beach **unless** *the rain stops.*

Second conditional

If clause	Main clause
past simple	*would* + infinitive (without *to*)

We use the second conditional to talk about the results of an action or a situation:

- that probably won't happen now or in the future.
It **would be** *cheaper if we* **stayed** *in a youth hostel.*

- that we know will not happen now or in the future.
If I **owned** *a yacht, I***'d sail** *around the world.*

We can also use the second conditional to give advice.
If I **were** *you, I***'d make** *a reservation soon.*

We can use *could* or *might* in the main clause instead of *would*.
*If you **went** to Canada, you **could** visit your cousins.*
*I **might** leave a tip if the waiters **were** friendlier.*

Third conditional

If clause	Main clause
past perfect	*would* + *have* + past participle

We can use *were* for all persons in
second conditional sentences.
*If I **were** you, I'd book tickets soon.*
*If Sophia **weren't** working, she'd come.*

We use the third conditional to talk about events or situations in the past that could have happened but didn't.
These are always hypothetical because we cannot change the past.
*If he **hadn't booked** so late, he **would have got** a cheaper ticket.*
(He booked late, so he didn't get a cheaper ticket.)

We can use *could* or *might* in the main clause instead of *would*.
*We **could have gone** to Australia if we **had had** more time.*
*If you **had run**, you **might have caught** the train!*

Mixed conditionals

If clause	Main clause
past perfect	*would* + infinitive (without *to*)

A mixed conditional is where the two clauses in a conditional sentence refer to different times. We use a mixed conditional to express the present result of a hypothetical past event or situation.
*If she **had left** earlier, she **would be** here already.*

Grammar exercises

2 Choose the correct option to complete the sentences.

1 When you arrive, they *check / would check* your passport.

2 I *would be / am* very angry if they lost my luggage.

3 If I *have / had* a dog, I'd call it Zeus.

4 You *would be / will be* fine if you don't panic.

5 If she *ate / is eating* more vegetables, she would be healthier.

6 I would have come with you if you *had bought / buy* me a ticket.

7 If you *arrive / arrived* late, you have to wait for the next train.

8 Try climbing if you *want / wanted* an exciting hobby.

9 If they hadn't missed that plane, they *would be / will be* in Italy now.

10 We could have won if we *had worked / work* together as a team.

3 Complete the sentences using the first conditional.

1 She _____ (like) it if you _____ (visit) her.

2 If you _____ (not / stop) shouting, you _____ (hurt) your throat.

3 We _____ (not / get) a seat on the train if we _____ (not / leave) now.

4 I _____ (carry) your suitcase for you if you _____ (feel) ill.

5 They _____ (be) angry if you _____ (not / tell) them about the accident.

6 If you _____ (not / know) where to go, you _____ (find) a map on the website.

7 If they _____ (like) your story, they _____ (publish) it.

8 He _____ (not / go) hiking in the mountains if it _____ (be) still raining.

4 Complete the sentences using the second conditional.

1 He trains very hard; that's why he is so fit.
If he _____ so hard, he _____ so fit.

2 She doesn't have to work at weekends, so she goes camping.
She _____ camping if she _____ work at weekends.

3 They get on well; that's why they travel together.
If they _____ well, they _____ together.

4 We go to bed early, so we get up easily the next day.
We _____ easily the next day if we _____ to bed early.

5 I can't drink this coffee because it's too hot.
If this coffee _____ so hot, I _____ drink it.

6 His phone isn't working, so he can't read his messages.
He _____ his messages if his phone _____ working.

7 They have parties every night, so they're tired every day.
If they _____ parties every night, they _____ tired every day.

8 He doesn't own a bike, so he doesn't cycle to work.
He _____ to work if he _____ a bike.

5 Complete the sentences using the third conditional.

1 If we _____ (not / buy) tickets, we _____ (not / be) allowed inside.

2 We _____ (bring) some food if we _____ (know) you didn't have any.

3 If I _____ (hear) that you were in town, I _____ (arrange) to meet you.

4 You _____ (not be) disappointed if you _____ (come) to the exhibition.

5 If he _____ (have) any more luggage, he _____ (have to) pay extra.

6 She _____ (not / see) the view if she _____ (not / sit) by the window.

7 If we _____ (know) it would make us ill, we _____ (not / eat) it.

8 I _____ (help) you if you _____ (ask) me.

6 Complete the sentences with the correct form of the verbs.

1 If you _____ (not / drink) so much coffee, you would feel fine now.

2 I _____ (have) some great photos now if I'd remembered my phone!

3 If they _____ (go) to New Zealand they wouldn't be with us today.

4 She _____ (not / be) in hospital now if she had been wearing a helmet.

5 If you had read the guidebook, you _____ (know) where to go.

6 We'd be lying on the beach now if we _____ (not / miss) the plane.

7 Dan would be able to speak Spanish if he _____ (start) learning when he was a boy.

8 If they hadn't spent a year in Rome, they _____ (not / know) Emilia and Seppe.

7 Find one mistake in each sentence. Then correct the mistakes.

1 If you will want to eat here tonight, you will need a reservation.

_____

2 The tickets would have been cheaper if you had book them online.

_____

3 If I was you, I would speak to her about it.

_____

4 We will be there now if we hadn't left so late.

_____

5 You can book your return ticket when you were there.

_____

6 If I had had more money, I'll stay in a hotel.

_____

7 She might have missed the flight if she wasn't set an alarm.

_____

8 If he hadn't forgotten his passport, he'll be here now.

_____

Vocabulary

Word formation

8 Match the words (1–8) with their meanings (a–h).

1 accommodate	☐	**a**	travel around
2 architect	☐	**b**	provide with a place to stay
3 board	☐	**c**	return to the ground after flying
4 depart	☐	**d**	allow
5 land	☐	**e**	get on a plane, boat, or train
6 mountain	☐	**f**	a person who designs buildings
7 permit	☐	**g**	a very high hill
8 tour	☐	**h**	leave

9 Use the word in capitals to form a word that fits in the gap.

1 The _____ in Barcelona is amazing.   **ARCHITECT**

2 The flight was very smooth and enjoyable, but the _____ was rough.   **LAND**

3 We need to find some _____ before it gets too late.   **ACCOMMODATE**

4 Do you have _____ to enter this area?   **PERMIT**

5 The west of Scotland is a very _____ area.   **MOUNTAIN**

6 Have you got our _____ passes? We should hurry.   **BOARD**

7 I hope our _____ is not delayed again.   **DEPART**

8 There are a lot of _____ visiting London at this time of year.   **TOUR**

Exam practice

Sentence transformation

10 Complete the second sentence so that it has a similar meaning to the first sentence, using the word given. Do not change the word given. You must use between two and five words.

1 You failed the test because you didn't study.

If _____, you wouldn't have failed the test.   **HAD**

2 My advice to you is – don't do it.

If _____, I wouldn't do it.   **WERE**

3 I didn't see her, so I didn't give her the message.
   If _____ , I would have given her the message.   SEEN

4 Tom can't drive, so he has to ride his bike everywhere.
   If Tom could drive, _____ ride his bike everywhere.   NOT

5 Wearing a helmet will reduce the chance of injury.
   You will reduce the chance of injury _____ a helmet.   IF

6 My phone isn't working, so I can't call you.
   If my phone _____ you.   COULD

7 Dad didn't go to the bank, so he didn't have any cash.
   Dad _____ if he had gone to the bank.   WOULD

8 She won't eat that because it has meat in it.
   She would eat that _____ meat in it.   HAVE

Multiple-choice cloze

11 **For questions 1–8, decide which answer (A, B, C or D) best fits each gap.**

1 If you recycle, you ___ protect the planet.
   A helping   **B** help   **C** helps   **D** helped

2 He ___ fall if he is not careful.
   A will   **B** would   **C** is   **D** has

3 If she ___ the address, she would tell you.
   A knows   **B** known   **C** knew   **D** know

4 We could have stayed longer if we had ___ time.
   A have   **B** having   **C** has   **D** had

5 If the town hadn't been destroyed, it would ___ be beautiful.
   A now   **B** still   **C** yet   **D** even

6 I ___ go to Costa Rica if I had more money.
   A would   **B** will   **C** have   **D** had

7 You could ___ caught the bus if you had run faster.
   A may   **B** have   **C** had   **D** might

8 I wouldn't tell him if I ___ you.
   A am   **B** was   **C** be   **D** were

Writing

12 **Complete these sentences in your notebook so that they are true for you.**

1 If I had a billion euros, …
2 I'd be very angry if …
3 If it's sunny this weekend, …
4 If I could live anywhere in the world, …
5 If I'd been born a hundred years ago, …
6 I'll laugh if …

Awareness

1 **Which of these sentences are correct (C) and incorrect (I)?**

1 If you hadn't eaten so much, you'll feel better now. ___

2 Provided everyone is ready, we'll leave at 5 p.m. ___

3 Supposing you could go anywhere, where would you go? ___

4 I wish we don't book a package tour. ___

5 We'll book a cruise, provided you could come too. ___

6 If only she spoke Spanish, she'd be able to help us. ___

7 Don't touch that, otherwise you might broke it. ___

8 They'll go on a road trip as long as the car is OK. ___

9 They won't be able to come otherwise they're too busy. ___

10 He wishes he has unpacked yesterday. ___

How many did you get right? ☐

Grammar

Conditionals without *if*

We can use *provided / providing (that)* and *as long as* to replace *if* in first conditional sentences.
Provided (that) the weather is good, we'll go on an excursion.
Providing (that) you have comfortable shoes, we'll explore the old city this afternoon.
As long as we catch the next bus, we'll get to the airport in time.

We can use *unless* in first and second conditional sentences. It means the same as *if not*.
We won't exchange money **unless** our credit card doesn't work.
Unless you make a reservation, you won't be able to eat here tonight.

We can use *otherwise* to replace an *if* clause. It means *if not*.
If you don't take your binoculars, you won't be able to see the birds.
Take your binoculars. **Otherwise**, you won't be able to see the birds.

We can use *supposing* in all conditional sentences. The main clause is often a question. It means *imagine / what if*.
Supposing his passport doesn't arrive, what will he do?
Supposing you hadn't seen the warning sign, what would have happened?
Supposing you were lost in a strange city, who would you call?

wish and *if only*

We use *wish* to talk about a situation or an action we aren't happy about, or to say how we would like something to be different.

We use *wish* + a past tense when we talk about the present or the future.
I wish I knew how to speak Mandarin.

We use *wish* + a past perfect tense when we talk about the past.
I wish the tour guide **had been** more helpful.

We use *wish* + *would* + infinitive without *to* when we talk about other people's annoying habits or to say that we would like something to be different in the future. We use it for actions, not states. We can only use *wish* + *would* when the subjects are different.
I wish they **wouldn't let** dogs into parks.
I wish the weather **would get** better.

We can use *if only* instead of *wish* in affirmative and negative sentences.
If only they hadn't cancelled the trip.
If only the youth hostel was closer to the centre.

Grammar exercises

2 **Choose the correct option to complete the sentences.**

1 You had better make a booking soon, *provided / unless / otherwise* it might sell out.
2 He won't go to the party *provided / unless / as long* as you go with him.
3 I'll help you unpack *as long as / unless / supposing* you help me with the washing.
4 *Providing / Supposing / Unless* it snows tomorrow, what should we do?
5 *Provided / Supposing / Unless* you've made a reservation, you can eat here.
6 She won't be happy *provided / otherwise / unless* we go to the museum.
7 We'll go to the beach tomorrow *providing / supposing / unless* the weather is good enough.
8 *As long as / Supposing / Providing* the campsite had been closed, where would you have stayed?

3 **Complete the second sentence so that it has a similar meaning to the first sentence.**

1 If you aren't ready, we won't leave.
Unless _____ .

2 If she doesn't have an umbrella, she'll get wet.
Unless _____ .

3 We won't go hiking in the mountains if it doesn't stop snowing.
Unless _____ .

4 If you don't leave now, you might miss your flight.
Unless _____ .

5 They won't come if you don't invite them.
Unless _____ .

6 I won't go on holiday if I don't feel better.
Unless _____ .

4 **Match the beginnings of the sentences (1–8) with the endings (a–h).**

1 You can play your music as long as	☐	a	he rides carefully.
2 I'll get a ticket for you provided	☐	b	I work on Sundays.
3 We can go to the beach if	☐	c	it doesn't rain.
4 They'll give me the job provided	☐	d	they have a big breakfast.
5 He can borrow my bike if	☐	e	you pay me back tomorrow.
6 I'll cook dinner as long as	☐	f	you play it quietly.
7 She doesn't have to finish it today provided	☐	g	she finishes it tomorrow.
8 They won't be hungry at lunchtime if	☐	h	you do the washing up.

5 **Choose the correct option to complete the sentences.**

1 I wish I *can / could* run faster.
2 I wish Simon *doesn't speak / didn't speak* so quickly.
3 She wishes she *learned / had learned* how to drive.
4 If only I could *stay / stayed* at the resort with you.
5 He really wishes he *didn't forget / hadn't forgotten* his wallet.
6 If only Mark *bought / had bought* that house two years ago.
7 I wish you *didn't say / hadn't said* anything about the surprise trip.
8 If only this beautiful weather *can / could* last a little bit longer.

6 Complete the sentences with the correct form of the verbs.

1 I wish I _____ (can) swim with dolphins.

2 My mum wishes she _____ (study) languages at school.

3 James wishes he _____ (not / run) to the bus stop – now he feels hot.

4 If only I _____ (have) more time to explore the historic parts of town.

5 I wish people _____ (tip) waiters more generously.

6 If only we _____ (not / lose) our passports.

7 I wish the tourists _____ (stop) arguing with the taxi driver.

8 My brother wishes he _____ (be) as good as me at map reading.

7 Complete the sentences with one word in each gap.

1 I _____ I could speak Portuguese.

2 He wouldn't cancel his trip _____ he really had to.

3 Provided _____ you download the app, you'll have no problem parking.

4 Supposing you were lost in the rainforest, how _____ you feel?

5 If _____ I had known about this place years ago.

6 You had better go to bed now, _____ you'll be exhausted in the morning.

7 She'll help you _____ that you ask her politely.

8 You can use my towel _____ long as you wash it afterwards.

Vocabulary

Phrasal verbs

8 Complete the phrasal verbs with these verbs. Some verbs can be used more than once.

check   drop   get   put   see   set

1 _____ around – move from place to place

2 _____ off – take someone somewhere and leave them

3 _____ in – arrive at a hotel

4 _____ on – board a plane or train

5 _____ off – begin a journey

6 _____ off – wave goodbye to someone leaving from an airport or a station

7 _____ up – assemble or build something

8 _____ away – escape

9 Complete the sentences with the correct form of the phrasal verbs from Exercise 8.

1 It's an old car, but it works fine for _____ me _____ town.

2 They _____ a new shopping mall next to the airport.

3 We _____ to the hotel just after midnight.

4 I won't come and _____ you _____ at the station tomorrow because I hate saying goodbye.

5 The taxi _____ us _____ in the city centre.

6 It will soon be time for us to _____ the plane.

7 I like to _____ from the big city every summer, and relax on a quiet island.

8 If we _____ at around 5 a.m., we'll get there before noon.

Exam practice

Sentence transformation

10 Complete the second sentence so that it has a similar meaning to the first sentence, using the word given. Do not change the word given. You must use between two and five words.

1 Dan forgot his passport and he regrets it.
Dan wishes _____ his passport. **FORGOTTEN**

2 I wish I could ride a motorbike.
If _____ ride a motorbike. **ONLY**

3 I'm sorry that you didn't tell me.
I wish _____ me. **TOLD**

4 She regrets not going on the excursion.
She _____ on the excursion. **WISHES**

5 It's a pity that you forgot to phone me.
If only _____ to phone me. **REMEMBERED**

6 If you don't frighten the bee, it won't sting you.
The bee won't sting you _____ don't frighten it. **LONG**

7 They won't let you in if you aren't wearing smart clothes.
They won't let you in _____ smart clothes. **UNLESS**

8 If I have time, I'll make a trip to my grandparents' village.
I'll make a trip to my grandparents' village _____ I have time. **THAT**

Word formation

11 Use the word in capitals to form a word that fits in the gap.

1 If you don't understand the menu, a _____ is available. **TRANSLATE**
2 The taxi driver was so _____ when we arrived. **HELP**
3 We found the hotel with _____ because the directions were so clear. **EASY**
4 The weather was bad but, _____ , the flight was very smooth and relaxing. **SURPRISE**
5 Given the _____ , I would travel for a year before going to university. **CHOOSE**
6 The temperature dropped _____ when the sun went down. **DRAMATIC**
7 We enjoyed the _____ out of the train window. **SCENE**
8 The view of the mountains was really _____ from our hotel balcony. **IMPRESS**

Writing

12 Read the writing task and write your answer in 140–190 words in an appropriate style.

You see an advert on an English-speaking website asking for articles. Write an article answering these questions:

Describe the most interesting journey you've ever been on.
- Where did you go?
- How did you travel?
- Why was it so interesting?

Grammar

1 **Rewrite the sentences in reported speech.**

1 'You can go to the cinema tomorrow,' she said to me.
She told me that _____ .

2 'We were feeling very relaxed,' they said.
They said that _____ .

3 'Do you have any sisters?' he asked me.
He asked me _____ .

4 'They are leaving next month,' he said.
He said that _____ .

5 'Last weekend we went to Edinburgh,' she said.
She said that _____ .

6 'What were you doing last night?' he asked me.
He asked me _____ .

7 'I have never seen this before,' she said.
She said that _____ .

8 'Did you enjoy your meal?' she asked them.
She asked them _____ .

2 **Complete the sentences with the correct form of the verbs.**

1 The police accused Mario of _____ (steal) a phone.

2 I told you _____ (not / open) that window!

3 He congratulated his friend on _____ (pass) all his exams.

4 She offered _____ (give) me a lift to the airport.

5 Why did you suggest _____ (come) here? It's boring!

6 Mum asked me _____ (unpack) the shopping.

7 Jake denied _____ (tell) my secret to everyone.

8 The teacher advised me _____ (take) extra Spanish lessons.

3 **Match the beginnings of the sentences (1–8) with the endings (a–h).**

1 If we're late, ☐
2 When you press this button, ☐
3 You wouldn't have enjoyed it ☐
4 If they were more adventurous, ☐
5 If I were you, ☐
6 She'd sing us a song ☐
7 If you'd eaten all of your breakfast, ☐
8 If I'd known you were coming, ☐

a I'd apologise immediately.
b they'd enjoy exploring new places.
c if she had her guitar with her.
d if you had gone on your own.
e the door opens.
f I'd have made you some lunch.
g you wouldn't be hungry now.
h we'll have to catch the next train.

4 Choose the correct option to complete the sentences.

1 She *said / told* that she worked shifts.

2 They insisted on *stay / staying* until the end.

3 We'll do it *provided / supposing* you agree.

4 *If only / Otherwise* she took her studies more seriously.

5 You'll feel better if you *take / will take* a walk in the park.

6 She asked me when I *decide / had decided* to apply for the job.

7 I wish I *were / would be* older.

8 *Supposing / Providing* you lived abroad, where would it be?

5 Complete the second sentence so that it has a similar meaning to the first sentence, using the word given.

1 I really regret not joining the swimming club.

   If _____ the swimming club.　ONLY

2 Dan forgot his wallet, so he can't buy anything.

   Dan wishes he _____ .　FORGOTTEN

3 We can't hear what the tour guide is saying.

   We wish _____ more loudly.　SPEAK

4 She's upset because she forgot her passport.

   If _____ her passport.　REMEMBERED

5 Our neighbours are making a lot of noise.

   I wish _____ so much noise.　WOULD

6 He wants to drive a car, but he doesn't know how.

   He wishes _____ a car.　KNEW

7 It's been raining all day, and it's making me unhappy.

   If only _____ today.　WOULD

8 I can't surf well.

   I wish _____ better.　COULD

6 Find the mistake in each sentence. Then correct the mistakes.

1 Supposing you broke your mum's laptop, what did you do?

   _____

2 You can swim in our pool if you'll come and visit us.

   _____

3 She told she had been exploring the old castle.

   _____

4 I didn't buy that bike if I were you.

   _____

5 He wishes he has a bigger suitcase.

   _____

6 You didn't remind me cancelling the booking.

   _____

Exam practice

7 For questions 1–8, read the text below. Use the word given in capitals at the end of some of the lines to form a word that fits in the gap in the same line. There is an example at the beginning (0).

No gain without pain

In these days of (0) _economic_ hardship, it is very difficult for charities to raise money.	ECONOMY
'Charity fatigue' means ordinary appeals have become (1) _____ ineffective	INCREASE
and new ways of raising money have to be dreamt up. News channels and websites, which	
employ many (2) _____ people, are playing an important role in developing these new	CREATE
ideas. For example, they regularly organise unusual or demanding expeditions for their	
journalists and other celebrities to take part in. The hope is that (3) _____ viewers and	WEALTH
readers will make large (4) _____ to the cause – and they frequently do!	DONATE

On one such expedition, a group of journalists, acting as a well-known news organisation's	
representatives, climbed Mount Everest. Details of how (5) _____ became more difficult	BREATH
during the climb were reported daily, together with (6) _____ accounts of how each	PERSON
member of the team was coping. As can be imagined, those participating went through a	
great deal of physical and (7) _____ suffering. And the readers were hooked!	PSYCHOLOGY
As the climb progressed, readers were more inspired to donate money. It appeared that they	
felt a greater (8) _____ to give money to the appeal as the climbers' suffering increased.	OBLIGE

8 For questions 9–16, read the text below and decide which answer (A, B, C or D) best fits each gap. There is an example at the beginning (0).

Flora and fauna at risk

(0) ___ many leading zoologists and botanists have expressed their concern about the preservation of endangered species, most of the measures taken to (9) ___ these species against extinction have had little effect.

From the sea bed to mountain slopes, tens of thousands of species have become extinct in the (10) ___ 300 years. Thousands have died out even before they have been (11) ___ . Many experts now believe that humankind has reached the point of no return.

The greatest threat to plants and animals is the destruction of the planet's rainforests. On (12) ___ , an area of forest the size of the UK is destroyed every year. (13) ___ regions are cleared every month, which means that animals have nothing to eat and birds have nowhere to (14) ___ .

CITES (Convention on International Trade in Endangered Species) is an agreement between governments who have (15) ___ on the responsibility of getting more than 1,000 species of animals and plants (16) ___ from international trade. This is a step in the right direction, but should they fail, the howl of the wolf may only appear in children's stories.

	A		B		C		D	
0	A	Nevertheless	B	However	C	Despite	(D)	Although
9	A	maintain	B	shield	C	conserve	D	protect
10	A	earlier	B	former	C	past	D	previous
11	A	found out	B	discovered	C	determined	D	invented
12	A	average	B	normal	C	standard	D	typical
13	A	Total	B	Full	C	Entire	D	Complete
14	A	fly	B	grow	C	nest	D	flock
15	A	taken	B	turned	C	worked	D	seen
16	A	avoided	B	banned	C	stopped	D	prevented

Grammar

9 For questions 1–10, choose the word or phrase that best completes the sentence.

1 The teacher told me ___ .
   A revise more
   B revising more
   C to revising more
   D to revise more

2 'Will you come out with us tonight?'
   'OK, ___ we don't come home too late. '
   A as long as
   B otherwise
   C supposing
   D unless

3 I wouldn't have remembered if you ___ me.
   A didn't remind
   B weren't reminding
   C hadn't reminded
   D haven't reminded

4 I'm tired. I ___ to bed so late.
   A only hadn't gone
   B wish I hadn't gone
   C wouldn't have gone
   D didn't have gone

5 The interviewer asked me ___ music.
   A did I like
   B would I liked
   C if I liked
   D do I like

6 'What are you cooking tonight?'
   'Nothing. You promised ___ to a restaurant!'
   A to take us
   B to have taken us
   C taking us
   D you took us

7 If I were you, I ___ so near the stage.
   A didn't sit
   B haven't sat
   C 'm not sitting
   D wouldn't sit

8 ___ everyone is comfortable, I'll begin.
   A Supposing
   B Otherwise
   C Provided
   D Unless

9 Tonya said ___ to basketball matches.
   A she enjoyed going
   B she enjoys to go
   C she's enjoying to go
   D she enjoyed go

10 Mum suggested ___ a holiday.
   A to book
   B booking
   C book
   D I had booked

Vocabulary

10 For questions 11–20, choose the word or phrase that best completes the sentence.

11 He got the ___ from his job because he was always late.
   A bag
   B shoe
   C sack
   D fire

12 I'm leaving my job. I've handed in my ___ .
   A notice
   B CV
   C sign
   D position

13 I'm working in a shop to get some ___ experience.
   A tail
   B detail
   C entail
   D retail

14 ___ behalf of everyone here, thank you.
   A In
   B On
   C By
   D At

15 In my ___ , you made the right decision.
   A opinion
   B brain
   C idea
   D thoughts

16 You can't ___ the plane with all that luggage.
   A mount
   B ride
   C board
   D climb

17 We were looking for ___ in the city centre.
   A accommodation
   B room
   C house
   D sleeping

18 I'll ___ you off at the station, if you like.
   A put
   B push
   C drop
   D carry

19 What time did you ___ in to your hotel?
   A make
   B check
   C sign
   D join

20 They're putting ___ a new building in town.
   A out
   B on
   C over
   D up

Unit 21

Awareness

1 Which of these sentences are correct (C) and incorrect (I)?

1 We love the house next to the lake. ___
2 That's the man whose lawyer was a thief. ___
3 The police, that are still looking for the suspect, have no clues. ___
4 This is the place when the crime happened. ___
5 I'll never forget the day our flat was burgled. ___
6 My uncle, which is a judge, is very clever. ___
7 We interviewed a man looked very suspicious. ___
8 I don't know the reason why she did that. ___
9 I watched a film which I didn't like it. ___
10 A pickpocket is a thief who steals things from people's pockets or bags. ___

How many did you get right? ☐

Grammar

Relative clauses: defining and non-defining

Relative clauses give more information about the subject or the object of a sentence. They are introduced by the following words (relative pronouns):

- *who* for people
- *which* for things
- *whose* to show possession
- *when* for time
- *where* for places
- *why* for reason

Defining relative clauses

This type of relative clause gives us information that we need to be able to understand who or what the speaker is talking about. We do not use commas to separate it from the rest of the sentence. We can use *that* instead of *who* and *which* in defining relative clauses.
*That's the bank **where the robbery took place**.*
*We met some people **who / that were very strange**.*

When *who*, *which*, *that*, *when* or *why* is the object of the relative clause, we can omit the relative pronoun.
*He was the actor (**who**) they chose to play the victim.*
*Do you remember the time (**when**) someone broke into the school?*

Non-defining relative clauses

This type of relative clause gives us extra information which isn't necessary to be able to understand the meaning of the main clause. We use commas to separate it from the rest of the sentence.
*My aunt, **who** lives in the same street as me, is a judge.*
*His essay, **which** is about prisons in the UK, is very informative.*

Grammar exercises

2 Choose the correct option to complete the sentences.

1 Is that the hotel *that / where* the suspect was staying?
2 The car, *which / who* was stolen last night, has already been found.
3 Do you remember the time *when / which* someone broke in to the school?
4 Mr Brown, *who / that* was staying with us at the time, had a lot of money.
5 You never told me the reason *which / why* you left work early.
6 My necklace, *which / that* I keep in a box in a drawer, is quite valuable.
7 Evening is the time *when / where* most crimes are committed.
8 There's the man *where / that* I was telling you about.

3 Complete the sentences with relative pronouns. Sometimes more than one answer is possible.

1   Murder is a crime _____ is very serious.

2   A detective is a police officer _____ solves crimes.

3   Is that the prison _____ the robbers are being held?

4   The day _____ Jack went to court was very stressful.

5   That's the boy _____ mother is a lawyer.

6   Do you know the reason _____ they released the prisoner?

7   It was a difficult case, _____ involved a lot of police work.

8   I don't know anyone _____ has been a member of a jury.

4 Can we leave the pronouns out of these sentences? Write yes (Y) or no (N).

1   The prisoners, who were in prison for five years, have been released.   ___

2   Can you remember the story that I told you?   ___

3   I met a boy whose sister was studying criminal law.   ___

4   The library where I usually study is closed today.   ___

5   The reason why Tom isn't at school is because he is ill.   ___

6   I'm thinking about that time when we all got lost in London.   ___

7   Did you see the man who stole your bag?   ___

8   The laptop which was found in the playground was not damaged.   ___

5 Match the beginnings of the definitions (1–8) with their endings (a–h). Complete with relative pronouns.

1   A victim is a person [ ]   a   _____ are used for fighting.

2   A prison is a place [ ]   b   _____ protects the head.

3   A helmet is a hat [ ]   c   _____ criminal trials happen.

4   A burglar is a criminal [ ]   d   _____ saw a crime.

5   A judge is a person [ ]   e   _____ job it is to sentence criminals.

6   Weapons are tools [ ]   f   _____ prisoners are kept.

7   A witness is a person [ ]   g   _____ is harmed as a result of a crime.

8   A court is a place [ ]   h   _____ steals from houses.

6 Join the sentences with a relative pronoun. Remember to add commas if the clause is non-defining.

1   Simon is a great teacher. His wife is a judge.
    Simon, whose wife is a judge, is a great teacher.

2   Lots of people break the law. They end up in prison.
    _____

3   Last winter is hard to forget. The playground was vandalised.
    _____

4   Your computer has been found in the library. You have been looking for it.
    _____

5   They're building a factory on the park. I used to play there as a boy.
    _____

6   Mrs Smith was a witness. Her son is in my class.
    _____

7 Find one mistake in each sentence. Then correct the mistakes.

1 My old school, where I went there for six years, has been burgled.

_____

2 Lots of people which own cars don't really need them.

_____

3 Do you know the reason why he was stopped by the police for?

_____

4 A colleague, mum is a police officer, was caught shoplifting.

_____

5 He married a girl who she was from Argentina.

_____

6 The phone you gave me it doesn't work.

_____

7 This skateboard, that I have had since I was seven, is my favourite object.

_____

8 The car who he bought last month has been stolen.

_____

Vocabulary

Collocations and expressions

8 Match 1–8 with a–h to form expressions.

1	be against		a	the law
2	be under		b	a fine
3	be under		c	investigation
4	break		d	arrest
5	criminal		e	record
6	let		f	a case
7	pay		g	someone off
8	solve		h	the law

9 Complete the sentences with the correct form of the expressions from Exercise 8.

1 I hoped that the judge would put him in prison, but she _____ him _____ .

2 If you are caught driving too fast, you might have to _____ .

3 The police asked them lots of questions while they were _____ .

4 Is it _____ to use a mobile phone while driving?

5 She had a _____ by the time she was fifteen.

6 Stop! You're _____ on suspicion of arson.

7 The detective was very happy when he finally _____ the _____ .

8 Do not _____ – there is a good chance that you will be caught.

Exam practice

Sentence transformation

10 Complete the second sentence so that it has a similar meaning to the first sentence, using the word given. Do not change the word given. You must use between two and five words.

1 Zoe is the girl with the very fast motorbike.

Zoe is the girl _____ very fast.　　**WHOSE**

2 We saw a robbery in the market.

The robbery _____ was in the market.　　**THAT**

3 Tom is very brave and is an excellent police officer.

Tom, _____ , is an excellent police officer.　　**WHO**

4 He never buys stolen property.

He never _____ stolen.　　**WHICH**

5 She's sleeping in a caravan by the beach.

The caravan _____ is by the beach.　　**WHERE**

6 One of my dogs is a Chihuahua.

I have _____ a Chihuahua.　　**WHICH**

7 We went to Spain last year – it's our favourite country.

Spain, _____ , is our favourite country.　　**WENT**

8 They'll never forget visiting the court.

They'll never forget the time _____ the court　　**VISITED**

Open cloze

11 Read the sentences and think of a word which best fits each gap. Use only one word in each gap.

1 That's the boy _____ father is a lawyer.

2 I have a friend _____ loves crime dramas.

3 There isn't much crime in the part of the city _____ I live.

4 The jewellery, _____ was quite expensive, was in a locked box.

5 There's the dog _____ bit me last week.

6 Can you think of a reason _____ I shouldn't come with you?

7 That boy, _____ hair is dyed blue, is in trouble!

8 Did you enjoy the film _____ I told you about?

Writing

12 Write sentences in your notebook which are true for you. Use relative clauses.

- a day you will never forget (when)
- an activity you would like to try (which / that)
- a famous person you would like to meet (who)
- a place you would like to go (where)

Awareness

1 **Which of these sentences are correct (C) and incorrect (I)?**

1 She found her cat hiding under the bed. ___
2 The boy was given a medal felt very proud. ___
3 Not knowing what time the film started, we set off early. ___
4 The people employing last month were really good. ___
5 Not know what to do, I phoned my dad. ___

6 Seen from a distance, that looks dangerous. ___
7 Watch the burglar being arrested, I felt relieved. ___
8 The woman speaking is my mother. ___
9 The boy punished for vandalism is thirteen. ___
10 They weren't happy with the prison sentence given to the thief. ___

How many did you get right? ☐

Grammar

Reduced relative clauses

A reduced relative clause is a defining relative clause that has been shortened. This is possible when the subject of the main sentence and the relative clause is the same. We shorten the relative clause by replacing the relative pronoun and verb in the relative clause with a participle form of the verb.

There are two kinds of participles. The present participle (verb + -ing) and the past participle (verb + -ed or irregular form). We use a present participle if the verb is active and a past participle if the verb is passive.
*The detectives **who solved** the case worked very hard.*
→*The detectives **solving** the case worked very hard.*

*The girl **who was caught** shoplifting had to pay a fine.*
→*The girl **caught** shoplifting had to pay a fine.*

We can use participles in the same way in participle clauses.
*Before **he left** the house, Nathan locked all the windows.*
→ *Before **leaving** the house, Nathan locked all the windows.*

*When **she was asked** if she knew the victim, she replied that she didn't.*
→ ***Asked** if she knew the victim, she replied that she didn't.*

Grammar exercises

2 **Choose the correct option to complete the sentences.**

1 I'd like to buy the jacket *displayed / displaying* in the window, please.
2 Not *been / being* able to find a taxi, we walked home.
3 The man *talking / who talking* to the police officer is my uncle.
4 *Caught / Catching* stealing sweets, the boy asked them to let him go.
5 All pupils *wanted / wanting* to study law must apply by the end of this week.
6 I hurt my arm *playing / played* volleyball.
7 The subjects *taught / teaching* in your school are different from in mine.
8 *Walked / Walking* through the park, I saw a pickpocket stealing a wallet.

3 Match sentences 1–8 with sentences a–h. Join them with an *-ing* clause.

1 Carla was in her bedroom. ☐   a She was chasing the thief.
2 Tom left the house on Friday. ☐   b They saw the girls leave without paying.
3 A woman was wearing a red coat. ☐   c He said he'd be back on Sunday.
4 The boys waited outside the classroom. ☐   d They had been sent out by the teacher.
5 The dog is running down the street. ☐   e We were cycling to school.
6 You don't have permission. ☐   f It has stolen some sausages!
7 Two people were eating in the café. ☐   g You will not be allowed inside.
8 We saw an accident yesterday. ☐   h She was doing her homework.

1 *Carla was in her bedroom doing her homework.*
2 _____
3 _____
4 _____
5 _____
6 _____
7 _____
8 _____

4 Rewrite the sentences with a present participle clause.

1 The woman who is running down the street has stolen my phone!
The woman running down the street has stolen my phone!

2 We didn't know the city, so we bought a map.
_____

3 I thought these were your headphones, so I brought them for you.
_____

4 The car that was speeding up the street was going in the wrong direction.
_____

5 Anyone who uses their phone in class will be punished.
_____

6 While she was sitting on her bed, she remembered something important.
_____

5 Rewrite the sentences with a past participle clause.

1 The man who was found innocent cried because he was happy.
The man found innocent cried because he was happy.

2 The teacher didn't know what to say when she was asked a grammar question.
_____

3 The woman who was sentenced to five years in prison will get out in 2026.
_____

4 The boy who was injured in the park was taken to hospital.
_____

5 Everyone loves Emily because she's very honest.
_____

6 English, which is spoken all over the world, is a useful language to learn.
_____

6 Complete the sentences with these verbs.

| bark | break | call | frighten | live | offer | study | work |

1 The kids were woken up by a dog _____ .

2 _____ in a flat, we don't have a garden.

3 Anyone _____ law at our school can go on the trip to the court.

4 The window _____ by the burglar has now been replaced.

5 _____ a job in a music shop, I was very happy.

6 A girl _____ Mia has sent you a text message.

7 The man _____ at the petrol station reported the crime.

8 _____ by the noise, the cat hid under the sofa.

7 Find one mistake in each sentence. Then correct the sentences. Use participle clauses.

1 Not know her phone number, I sent her an email.

_____

2 The woman who singing on the stage is my mum.

_____

3 The man that arrested was questioned by the police for five hours.

_____

4 Anyone finding in the building without permission will be asked to leave.

_____

5 Think the children might be hungry, I made some sandwiches.

_____

6 The police officer was call to the scene interviewed two witnesses.

_____

Vocabulary

Prepositions

8 Complete the phrases with these prepositions. Some prepositions can be used more than once.

| for | through | to | with |

1 be familiar _____

2 be halfway _____

3 be responsible _____

4 be similar _____

5 pay attention _____

6 rush _____

7 vote _____

8 work _____

9 Complete the sentences with the correct form of the phrases from Exercise 8.

1 Police officers _____ doctors to help the victim.

2 This story is quite _____ the one you read to us last week.

3 Who is _____ breaking the window?

4 Are you _____ the fictional detective Sherlock Holmes?

5 I was _____ the book when I decided to give up – it was so boring!

6 Detectives had to _____ every detail to help them solve the case.

7 She _____ reading the report so that she could go home early.

8 Who did you _____ in the last election?

Exam practice

Sentence transformation

10 Complete the second sentence so that it has a similar meaning to the first sentence, using the word given. Do not change the word given. You must use between two and five words.

1 I didn't understand the word, so I looked it up in the dictionary.

Not _____ , I looked it up in the dictionary.   **UNDERSTANDING**

2 Not being hungry, the children left the table.

The children left the table _____ hungry.   **BECAUSE**

3 The lessons that Mr Brown teaches have been cancelled.

The lessons _____ have been cancelled.   **TAUGHT**

4 Hurt by the accusations, Miriam didn't go outside for a month.

Miriam, _____ the accusations, didn't go outside for a month.   **WHO**

5 Do you know the rules of chess?

Are _____ the rules of chess?   **FAMILIAR**

6 Who is in charge of deciding prison sentences?

Who _____ deciding prison sentences?   **RESPONSIBLE**

7 My taste in films is almost the same as my sister's taste in films.

My sister's taste in films _____ mine.   **TO**

8 You have to concentrate carefully on the question to get the right answer.

You have to _____ the question to get the right answer.   **ATTENTION**

Word formation

11 Use the word in capitals to form a word that fits in the gap.

1 Don't worry, _____ crime isn't very common here.   VIOLENCE

2 Did you notice any strange _____ last night?   BEHAVE

3 There's been a _____ at my brother's school.   BURGLAR

4 Was the suspect found innocent or _____ ?   GUILT

5 I'll wait for you at the _____ to the police station.   ENTER

6 I don't think _____ is as serious as arson.   VANDAL

7 Police were shocked to find a _____ of weapons.   VARY

8 Did you know that he had a _____ record?   CRIME

Writing

12 Read the writing task and write your answer in 140–190 words in an appropriate style.

Allowing criminals to meet their victims can be more effective in preventing crime than a prison sentence.

- Write an **essay** discussing the advantages and disadvantages of this idea.
- Include specific reasons and details to support your opinion.

Awareness

1 **Which of these sentences are correct (C) and incorrect (I)?**

1 We have had the hall redecorated. ___
2 Have you have had your hearing tested? ___
3 What time are you have your car fixed? ___
4 She's having her hair cut at the moment. ___
5 We got our house burgled last week. ___

6 Are you getting your suit cleaning? ___
7 Have you ever had your computer checked? ___
8 I lost my certificate, but had got it replaced. ___
9 They'll have their photos taken by Sara. ___
10 How often do you getting your nails done? ___

How many did you get right? ☐

Grammar

Causative

We use the causative:
- to say that someone has arranged for someone to do something for them.
*Ellen is **having** some jewellery **designed.***
- to say that something unpleasant happened to someone.
*I **had** my watch **stolen** last week.*

We form the causative with *have* + object + past participle.
It can be used in a variety of tenses.
When we want to mention the agent, we use the word *by*.
*We **have had** new carpets **fitted.***
*My grandmother **used to have** her hair **styled** every week.*
*I'**m going to have** my teeth **checked** by the dentist.*

> ### Note
> We can also use *get* + object + past participle. This structure is less formal. However, when we talk about unpleasant events, we must use *have*.
> *I **got** my computer **repaired** in the shop across the road.*

Grammar exercises

2 **Choose the correct option to complete the sentences.**

1 Did you get the presents *wrap / wrapped* in the shop?
2 I'm *get / getting* my trousers shortened.
3 He *has had / had* his jacket dry cleaned yesterday.
4 Are you going to *have / got* your boots repaired?
5 It's a long time since we had our car *wash / washed*.
6 Jane *had / got* her finger broken playing basketball.
7 You must *get / to have* your eyes tested soon.
8 Where do you usually *have / got* your hair cut?

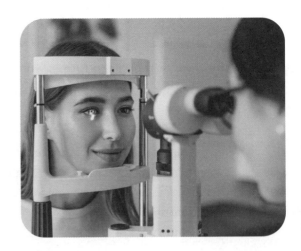

3 **Complete the sentences with the correct form of the causative.**

1 We _____ only once since we bought it. (the swimming pool / fill)
2 They _____ when I visited them. (the garden / tidy)
3 I _____ (already / my bag / steal) by the time I checked in.
4 He _____ at the moment. (his bike / fix)
5 We _____ last week. (our front door / paint)
6 Ron _____ every three years. (his car / replace)

4 Rewrite the sentences using the causative.

1 Someone stole her handbag.
She _____ .

2 He's polishing my shoes.
I _____ .

3 Someone broke into my uncle's car.
My uncle _____ .

4 The baker is going to make a birthday cake for me tomorrow.
I'm _____ .

5 A mechanic fixed Alex's car for him.
Alex _____ .

6 The fashion students are making out team t-shirts.
We're _____ .

7 Tomorrow, someone is going to build a website for me.
I _____ .

8 Last month some photos were taken of us.
We _____ .

5 Write answers to the questions using the causative.

1 Does he cut his own hair?
No, _____ *he has / gets it cut by his cousin* _____ . (his cousin)

2 Are you going to pack all these boxes?
No, _____ . (by a removal company)

3 Did they design this website themselves?
No, _____ . (a web designer)

4 Will you and your friend print your designs yourselves?
No, _____ . (by our friend Zak)

5 Is she going to make her own suit?
No, _____ . (by a tailor)

6 Do you dye your own hair?
No, _____ . (by a hairdresser)

6 Write questions for the answers using the causative.

1 *Who did you have your spotted shirt designed by?*   I had my spotted shirt designed by Mario.

2 _____   I had my teeth examined last week.

3 _____   I need to get my trousers repaired.

4 _____   I get my mum to help with my maths homework.

5 _____   I have my eyes tested every two years.

6 _____   I had my stripy dress made in Turkey.

7 **Find one mistake in each sentence. Then correct the mistakes.**

1 Anna got her mobile phone stolen last night.

_____

2 Did you had your boots mended?

_____

3 Grandad is have his shopping delivered this evening.

_____

4 We always have presents wrap in the shop.

_____

5 How often do you getting your hair styled?

_____

6 I hope you will getting that jacket cleaned soon.

_____

Vocabulary

Phrasal verbs

8 **Complete the phrasal verbs with these prepositions. Some prepositions can be used more than once.**

in	on	up	with

1 do _____   – fasten with a zip or button
2 dress _____   – wear smart clothes
3 go _____   – match or look good with another item of clothing
4 mix _____   – put clothes together in an unusual way
5 take _____   – make clothes smaller and tighter
6 take _____   – shorten a piece of clothing
7 throw _____   – put on an item of clothing quickly or casually
8 wrap _____   – wear enough clothes if it's very cold

9 **Complete the sentences with the correct form of the verbs from Exercise 8.**

1 Those trousers are too long. I'll have them _____ .
2 Don't forget to _____ – it's cold outside today!
3 Do you think these trainers _____ these jeans?
4 You should _____ that coat because it's very windy today.
5 It was such an expensive hotel that we had to _____ for dinner.
6 Dan has lost a lot of weight, and has had to have all his trousers _____ .
7 I was in a hurry, so I just _____ the first jacket I saw.
8 Liz doesn't like all her clothes to look the same. She likes to _____ different styles.

Exam practice

Sentence transformation

10 **Complete the second sentence so that it has a similar meaning to the first sentence, using the word given. Do not change the word given. You must use between two and five words.**

1 Someone has already stolen three pens from me.
   I've _____ from me.   **HAD**

2 An engineer came to fix our washing machine.

We _____ by an engineer.　　　　**GOT**

3 The clothes need to be designed before we can make them.

You must _____ before we can make them.　　　　**DESIGNED**

4 Tom's dad always checks his homework for him.

Tom _____ by his dad.　　　　**GETS**

5 Is someone picking up the children from school for you?

Are you _____ from school for you?　　　　**HAVING**

6 They'll send Max his new glasses next week.

Max will _____ next week.　　　　**DELIVERED**

7 Their uniforms are washed every day because they get so dirty.

They _____ every day because they get so dirty.　　　　**HAVE**

8 They're going to build a new wardrobe for us tomorrow.

Tomorrow we're going to _____ for us.　　　　**BUILT**

Multiple-choice cloze

11 **For questions 1–8, decide which answer (A, B, C or D) best fits each gap.**

1 What time are you going to ___ your suit fitted?

　A have　　　　**B** getting　　　　**C** got　　　　**D** had

2 They had all their children ___ how to play an instrument.

　A teach　　　　**B** learnt　　　　**C** taught　　　　**D** teaching

3 I can't do ___ my jeans – they're too tight!

　A off　　　　**B** up　　　　**C** over　　　　**D** out

4 Does this top ___ with these trousers?

　A mix　　　　**B** dress　　　　**C** do　　　　**D** go

5 Hurry up! We need to leave now, so just throw ___ a clean t-shirt.

　A with　　　　**B** on　　　　**C** off　　　　**D** up

6 It was freezing, so the children were ___ up in warm coats, hats and gloves.

　A made　　　　**B** taken　　　　**C** mixed　　　　**D** wrapped

7 If the dress is too long, I'll have it taken ___ by my aunt.

　A up　　　　**B** out　　　　**C** over　　　　**D** down

8 You don't have to ___ up to eat here – it's not that formal.

　A make　　　　**B** work　　　　**C** dress　　　　**D** wake

Writing

12 **Imagine you could have six things done for you by someone else. In your notebook, write six sentences.**

I would have all my clothes made for me by a top fashion designer.

Unit 24

1 Which of these sentences are correct (C) and incorrect (I)?

1 Not only I do love eating pizzas, but I also cook them! —
2 It's time you have a bath. —
3 Never have I heard such a funny story. —
4 Under no circumstances you can borrow my shoes. —
5 The time's high I bought some new clothes. —

6 It's about time I taught you to dance. —
7 Under no circumstances are you allowed to enter this room. —
8 I've never been to such a boring lecture. —
9 Not only is it very expensive, but it also is ugly. —
10 It's time I went home. —

How many did you get right? ☐

Grammar

Inversion: *never*, *under no circumstances* and *not only ... but also*

We can use *never*, *under no circumstances*, and *not only ... but also* at the beginning of a sentence for emphasis. When we do this, the word order changes in the same way as for a question. This is called inversion.
I have never worn a floral dress.
Never have I worn a floral dress.

Jake not only collects trainers, he designs them.
Not only does Jake collect trainers, **but** he also designs them.

You are not allowed to take photographs here under any circumstances.
Under no circumstances are you allowed to take photographs here.

It's (about / high) time

We can use *it's time*, *it's about time* and *it's high time* + past tense to talk about something that should have already been done in the present.
It's time you **stopped** leaving your clothes on the floor.
It's about time I **started** work on my project.
It's high time he **learned** to wash his own clothes.

Grammar exercises

2 Choose the correct option to complete the sentences.

1 Never *had she / she had* seen such amazing jewellery.
2 Not only do I play football, *and / but* I also play tennis.
3 Under no circumstances *should you / you should* touch that machine.
4 It's time you *make / made* up your own mind.
5 Not only *designs he / does he design* his own clothes, but he also teaches fashion design.
6 Under no circumstances *are they allowed / they are allowed* to use their phones in class.
7 It's about time Amelia *does / did* some work.
8 Never have I *worn / wore* such a beautiful dress.

3 Join the sentences with *Not only … but also.*

1 We bought some new clothes. We also bought new shoes.

_____

2 She likes to play volleyball. She's also a good footballer.

_____

3 They had been visiting the exhibition. They had had lunch too.

_____

4 My cat is very pretty. It has a nice personality, too.

_____

5 The weather was very hot, and I was very thirsty.

_____

6 This project is going to take a long time, and it's not going to be very useful.

_____

7 We sell books and we also have a café where you can read them.

_____

8 That film was both exciting and funny.

_____

4 Invert the sentences.

1 Students may not, under any circumstances, use their mobile phones in the exam.
Under no _____ .

2 He has never wanted anything so much in his life.
Never _____ .

3 You're not allowed to park here under any circumstances.
Under _____ .

4 She had never met anyone so creative before.
Never _____ .

5 I rarely wear high heels these days.
Rarely _____ .

6 Children cannot, under any circumstances, enter the sauna.
Under no _____ .

7 I've seldom regretted doing anything in my life.
Seldom _____ .

8 You should not tell Eva about this under any circumstances.
Under no _____ .

5 Choose the correct option (a–c) to complete the sentences.

1 ___ have I paid so much for a pair of sunglasses!
   a Never   b It's time   c Not only

2 ___ I changed into more comfortable shoes.
   a Rarely   b Under no circumstances   c It's time

3 ___ can we exchange clothes without a receipt.
   a It's high time   b Not only   c Under no circumstances

4 ___ did I suspect that Freddie was a fashion designer.
   a Not only   b Never   c Seldom

5 ___ was that a silly thing to do, it was also selfish.
   a Seldom   b Not only   c It's high time

6 ___ can we afford to eat in a restaurant.
   a Seldom   b Not only   c It's about time

6 Write sentences with *It's time ...* and one of these verbs.

| build | clean | go | learn | leave | start | tell | wake up |

1 Jake can't tie his shoe laces.
   It's time he learned.

2 Sarah hasn't been to the dentist's for three years.

3 Mark hasn't started his project yet.

4 Alice's football boots have been very dirty for weeks.

5 Greg still doesn't know about the party.

6 There's still no sports centre in my town.

7 It's late, but these people are still here.

8 It's one o'clock in the afternoon and Dan is still asleep.

7 Find one mistake in each sentence. Then correct the mistakes.

1 Not only do I play the guitar, but also I sing.

_____

2 Under no circumstances you are allowed to drive this car.

_____

3 Never had she saw such an untidy room.

_____

4 It's time we go.

_____

5 Never I have made my own clothes.

_____

6 Not only is it cheap, it also is rather pretty.

_____

7 It's time about you washed that jacket.

_____

8 Under no circumstances we can give you a refund.

_____

Vocabulary

Word formation

8 Match the words (1–8) with their meanings (a–h).

1	beauty	☐	a	not complicated; easy to understand or do
2	collect	☐	b	a precious stone used to decorate the body or an object
3	exclusive	☐	c	a belief or custom that has existed for a long time
4	jewel	☐	d	to bring a group of things together
5	long	☐	e	not shared with another thing or person
6	simple	☐	f	the quality of being attractive or pleasing to the senses
7	style	☐	g	measuring a big distance
8	tradition	☐	h	a particular design of clothing

9 Use the word in capitals to form a word that fits in the gap.

1 You have a very nice _____ of shoes here.   **COLLECT**

2 We sold our story _____ to one newspaper.   **EXCLUSIVE**

3 Daniel always wears such _____ clothes.   **STYLE**

4 I love getting unusual _____ as a present.   **JEWEL**

5 She looks really _____ in that dress.   **BEAUTY**

6 _____ , Indian women wear red saris on their wedding day.   **TRADITION**

7 The _____ designs are sometimes the most attractive.   **SIMPLE**

8 Do you have any shorter trousers, or are they all the same _____ ?   **LONG**

24

Exam practice

Sentence transformation

10 Complete the second sentence so that it has a similar meaning to the first sentence, using the word given. Do not change the word given. **You must use between two and five words.**

1 I never want to go to that shop again.

Never _____ go to that shop again. **DO**

2 Emma hasn't tidied her room for months – she should.

It's _____ her room. **ABOUT**

3 You should never stroke a dog you do not know.

Under _____ a dog you do not know. **CIRCUMSTANCES**

4 Jon is handsome and clever.

Not only _____ , but he is also clever. **ONLY**

5 She had never bought clothes from a charity shop before.

Never _____ clothes from a charity shop before. **SHE**

6 You really ought to start revising for your exams.

It's _____ revising for your exams. **HIGH**

7 You must never take something from a shop without paying.

Under _____ something from a shop without paying. **SHOULD**

8 They design the t-shirts and they print them too.

_____ the t-shirts, but they also print them. **NOT**

Open cloze

11 Read the sentences and think of a word which best fits each gap. Use only one word in each gap.

1 It's about _____ you got up.

2 Under _____ circumstances can you borrow my new jacket.

3 Never _____ I seen such beautiful fabrics.

4 Not _____ did she buy a new skirt, but she also bought a top.

5 Rarely _____ we have time to go window shopping.

6 It's about time we _____ home.

7 Hardly _____ have I bought such expensive shoes.

8 Not only were the shoes back in stock, _____ I also got a discount.

Writing

12 Read the writing task and write your answer in 140–190 words in an appropriate style.

You see an announcement on your college website asking for reviews of clothes shops or clothing websites. Write a review of one that you particularly like or dislike. Include information on the type of clothes it sells, the prices, the services, and a recommendation.

Grammar

1 **Join the sentences with a relative pronoun. Use defining and non-defining relative clauses.**

   1 Gina is a good footballer. Her dad used to play for Arsenal.

   _____

   2 The concert was wonderful. Everyone was dancing there.

   _____

   3 The jacket has been sold. You wanted it.

   _____

   4 They're closing the market. I used to go there every week.

   _____

   5 Daniel is my best friend. His mother is the head teacher at my school.

   _____

   6 Oscar has a new bike. He has always loved cycling.

   _____

2 **Rewrite the sentences with a present or past participle clause.**

   1 He doesn't have a driving licence, so he can't hire a car.

   _____

   2 Clothes that were made in the 1950s were very stylish.

   _____

   3 He was annoyed when the waiter asked him to change tables.

   _____

   4 The wallet that was left on the bus was empty.

   _____

   5 The man who stole the bag ran towards the station.

   _____

   6 Anyone who uses a phone in class will be asked to put it away.

   _____

3 **Complete the sentences using the causative.**

   1 We _____ at the studio this afternoon. (our photo / take)

   2 He _____ yet. (not / his car / service)

   3 Did she _____ by a professional? (the website / design)

   4 We _____ twice last year. (house / burgle)

   5 Steve _____ yesterday. (his phone / steal)

   6 Do you _____ every time you enter a new country? (your passport / stamp)

   7 Will you _____ by tomorrow? (your computer / repair)

   8 My friend _____ when I called him. (his hair / cut)

4 **Choose the correct option (a–c) to complete the sentences.**

1 Not only ___ stylish, but it's also very cheap.
   a this shirt is   **b** is this shirt   **c** this shirt was

2 Never ___ a cold drink so much!
   a I hadn't enjoyed   **b** I had enjoyed   **c** had I enjoyed

3 It's high time you ___ to drive.
   a learned   **b** have learned   **c** did learn

4 Under no circumstances ___ my credit card!
   a you use   **b** you can use   **c** can you use

5 Never ___ such a colourful dress.
   a have I seen   **b** I have seen   **c** I saw

6 Not only ___ a house in the country, but he also has a flat in the city.
   a has he   **b** does he have   **c** he does have

7 It's about time we ___ some warmer weather.
   a have had   **b** had   **c** have

8 Under no circumstances ___ the pool at night.
   a they should use   **b** they shouldn't use   **c** should they use

5 **Choose the correct option to complete the sentences.**

1 My mum, *who / that* is a very good cook, has made a cake.
2 We found the children *hide / hiding* in the treehouse.
3 You should *get / to have* your eyes tested!
4 Never *had he / he had* worn such an expensive suit.
5 It's high time you *do / did* your homework.
6 Sam *had / got* his leg broken when he was ice-skating.
7 *Running / Ran* home after school, I met Charlie.
8 Early morning is the time *when / where* we take the dogs to the park.

6 **Find one mistake in each sentence. Then correct the mistakes.**

1 Dad's university, where he studied there for four years, is in Manchester.

___

2 The driver that stopped by the police was wearing a checked shirt.

___

3 I'm have my shoes repaired in the morning.

___

4 Not only is this the prettiest, it also is the least expensive.

___

5 Thought it was going to rain, I took my umbrella with me.

___

6 We got our clothes stolen while we were swimming in the sea.

___

7 My aunt, that is a police officer, is coming to stay with us.

___

8 It's time you go to school.

___

Exam practice

7 For questions 1–8, read the text below and think of a word which best fits each gap. Use only one word in each gap. There is an example at the beginning (0).

The ozone layer

The ozone layer, **(0)** __*which*__ consists **(1)** _____ a thin band of ozone gas high above the Earth's surface, is extremely important to life on our planet. **(2)** _____ is this thin layer of gas that protects life on Earth from the harmful, ultra-violet light which comes from the sun.

Since the 1960s, scientists have observed 'holes' in the ozone layer and done research **(3)** _____ the phenomenon. The holes **(4)** _____ caused by CFCs – chemicals which **(5)** _____ destroy huge amounts of ozone. CFCs are released into the atmosphere when refrigerators are destroyed and when aerosol sprays are used.

The results of the damage which has been **(6)** _____ to the ozone layer have been known for a number of years. Ultra-violet light kills plant life, reducing **(7)** _____ amount of oxygen in the atmosphere. Also, skin cancer is becoming more common.

Nowadays, however, fridges and sprays are not normally made with harmful CFCs in them. Destruction of the ozone layer has slowed considerably in recent years, and scientists are starting to see evidence that it **(8)** _____ recover in the next 30–50 years.

8 For questions 9–16, read the text below. Use the word given in capitals at the end of each line to form a word that fits in the gap in the same line. There is an example at the beginning (0).

The sound of music

Thanks to the latest **(0)** __*developments*__ in dairy farming, there is a new sound **DEVELOP**
to be heard on the grassy slopes of **(9)** _____ Europe. Early in the morning, **CENTRE**
(10) _____ of the sparsely populated agricultural regions of Austria and Southern **INHABIT**
Germany wake up to romantic melodies being played ... to cows! The effect of music on
mood has been widely researched and documented. However, never has it been put to such
(11) _____ use as it has in this case. The farmers are keen to make the lives of their **PRACTICE**
animals as calm and **(12)** _____ as possible. They claim that the music brightens up the **PEACE**
animals' day by allowing them to relax. Not only does this **(13)** _____ **SUBSTANTIAL**
increase the amount of milk produced, but it also helps the cows give it up much more easily.

To their **(14)** _____ , farmers have also found that the quality of milk is better. **ASTONISH**
With such **(15)** _____ results, it's not surprising that agriculturalists are now **REMARK**
broadening the scope of their experiments. Plans are currently being made to see how
(16) _____ music is in getting other farm animals to become more productive. **EFFECT**

Grammar

9 For questions 1–10 choose the word or phrase that best completes the sentence.

1 Never ___ such a clear explanation!
   A I have heard
   B I had heard
   C have I heard
   D had I heard

2 'Nice hair. Did you cut it yourself?'
   'No, I ___ by my nephew.'
   A cut it
   B got it
   C had it cut
   D it had cut

3 The girl ___ is my cousin.
   A singing
   B who sing
   C who singing
   D sings

4 The hotel ___ was terrible.
   A we stayed
   B where we stayed
   C that we stayed
   D we were staying

5 It's ___ your homework!
   A about time did you
   B high did you time
   C high time you did
   D time about you did

6 'My computer still isn't working.'
   'I thought you ___ last week.'
   A were fixed
   B had fixed
   C it had fixed
   D had it fixed

7 I hurt my leg ___ basketball.
   A to play
   B played
   C playing
   D play

8 They're destroying the library ___ .
   A I used to study
   B that I used to study
   C I used to study there
   D where I used to study

9 ___ to see the stage, we left the theatre.
   A Not being able
   B Being not able
   C Able not
   D Not been able

10 Under no circumstances ___ during the test.
   A you allowed to talk
   B are you allowed to talk
   C you are allowed to talk
   D allowed are you to talk

Vocabulary

10 For questions 11–20 choose the word or phrase that best completes the sentence.

11 I hope the thief is ___ arrest by now.
   A under
   B over
   C in
   D with

12 You should ___ up your coat – it's cold!
   A make
   B put
   C wrap
   D do

13 He had to pay a ___ of £200.
   A case
   B fine
   C law
   D crime

14 I'm not familiar ___ the rules of this game.
   A in
   B on
   C with
   D to

15 I can't believe they let the thief ___ with a fine.
   A off
   B away
   C out
   D from

16 Those trainers are similar ___ mine.
   A with
   B for
   C through
   D to

17 I need a top to ___ with these jeans.
   A do
   B go
   C mix
   D make

18 If you ___ the law, you'll be arrested.
   A break
   B hurt
   C snap
   D damage

19 I gave up on the book when I was halfway ___ it – it was so boring!
   A in
   B over
   C through
   D past

20 Will we have to ___ up smartly for the party?
   A dress
   B throw
   C do
   D take

Irregular verbs

Infinitive	Past simple	Past participle
be	was/were	been
beat	beat	beaten
become	became	become
begin	began	begun
bite	bit	bitten
blow	blew	blown
break	broke	broken
bring	brought	brought
broadcast	broadcast	broadcast
build	built	built
burn	burned / burnt	burned / burnt
buy	bought	bought
can	could	–
catch	caught	caught
choose	chose	chosen
come	came	come
cost	cost	cost
cut	cut	cut
deal	dealt	dealt
dig	dug	dug
do	did	done
draw	drew	drawn
dream	dreamed / dreamt	dreamed / dreamt
drink	drank	drunk
drive	drove	driven
eat	ate	eaten
fall	fell	fallen
feed	fed	fed
feel	felt	felt
fight	fought	fought
find	found	found
fly	flew	flown
forecast	forecast	forecast
forget	forgot	forgotten
get	got	got
give	gave	given
go	went	gone
grow	grew	grown
hang	hung	hung
have	had	had
hear	heard	heard
hide	hid	hidden
hit	hit	hit
hold	held	held
hurt	hurt	hurt
keep	kept	kept
know	knew	known
lead	led	led
learn	learned / learnt	learned / learnt
leave	left	left
lend	lent	lent
let	let	let
lie	lay	lain

Irregular verbs

Infinitive	Past simple	Past participle
light	lit	lit
lose	lost	lost
may	might	–
mean	meant	meant
make	made	made
meet	met	met
pay	paid	paid
prove	proved	proven
put	put	put
read	read (pronounced /red/)	read (pronounced /red/)
ride	rode	ridden
ring	rang	rung
rise	rose	risen
run	ran	run
say	said	said
see	saw	seen
sell	sold	sold
send	sent	sent
set	set	set
shake	shook	shaken
shine	shone	shone
show	showed	shown
shoot	shot	shot
shut	shut	shut
sing	sang	sung
sink	sank	sunk
sit	sat	sat
sleep	slept	slept
slide	slid	slid
smell	smelled / smelt	smelled / smelt
speak	spoke	spoken
speed	sped	sped
spend	spent	spent
spread	spread	spread
stand	stood	stood
steal	stole	stolen
stick	stuck	stuck
stink	stank	stunk
sweep	swept	swept
swim	swam	swum
take	took	taken
teach	taught	taught
tell	told	told
think	thought	thought
throw	threw	thrown
understand	understood	understood
wake	woke	woken
wear	wore	worn
win	won	won
write	wrote	written
win	won	won
write	wrote	written

Phrasal verbs

ask around	=	speak to several different people to try and get some information	(U11)
back out	=	decide not to do something you had arranged to do	(U8)
back up	=	save a copy of your work	(U8)
be into	=	be very interested in	(U3)
bring over	=	take someone or something to a place	(U15)
bring up	=	start discussing a subject	(U15)
burn down	=	destroy something, usually a building, with fire	(U11)
call back	=	return a phone call	(U15)
call in	=	visit someone	(U15)
catch on	=	become popular or fashionable	(U15)
catch up	=	talk to someone you haven't seen for a while and find out their news	(U15)
come across	=	find something by chance	(U3)
come up with	=	think of and create something new	(U8)
date back to	=	come from a time in the past	(U11)
die out	=	become extinct or disappear	(U11)
dig up	=	remove something from the ground	(U11)
do up	=	fasten with a zip or button	(U23)
dress up	=	wear smart clothes	(U23)
find out	=	discover a fact or information	(U3)
go with	=	match or look good with another item of clothing	(U23)
hang on	=	wait or be patient	(U15)
hang up	=	end a phone call	(U15)
log in	=	gain access to a computer	(U8)
look at	=	think carefully about something in order to make a decision	(U15)
look into	=	try to discover the facts about something	(U3)
look up	=	search for information	(U15)
make out	=	manage to see something which is difficult to see	(U3)
make up	=	say something that isn't true	(U3)
mix up	=	put clothes together in an unusual way	(U23)
pass down	=	give knowledge to a younger generation	(U11)
plug in	=	connect to an electricity supply or another piece of equipment	(U8)
put off	=	discourage	(U11)
rely on	=	trust or have confidence in someone or something	(U3)
set up	=	prepare or organise	(U8)
shut down	=	stop a machine or computer from working	(U8)
switch on	=	turn on a machine or light by pressing a button	(U8)
take in	=	make clothes smaller and tighter	(U23)
take off	=	become quickly successful	(U11)
take up	=	shorten a piece of clothing	(U23)
throw on	=	put on an item of clothing quickly or casually	(U23)
work out	=	find an answer or solution to something	(U3)
wrap up	=	wear enough clothes if it's very cold	(U23)

Prepositions

(be) different **from**	(U14)	**in** my opinion	(U18)
(be) familiar **with**	(U22)	**in** my spare time	(U2)
(be) good **at**	(U9)	laugh **at**	(U2)
(be) halfway **through**	(U22)	live **on**	(U14)
(be) **in** debt	(U18)	make a success **of**	(U9)
(be) out **of** work	(U18)	nervous **about**	(U2)
(be) **over** (years old)	(U5)	**on** behalf of	(U18)
(be) responsible **for**	(U22)	pay attention **to**	(U22)
(be) similar **to**	(U22)	prevent **from**	(U14)
(be) surprised **at**	(U9)	protect **against**	(U5)
(be) surprised **by**	(U14)	reach the top **of**	(U18)
a member **of**	(U5)	react **to** something	(U18)
according **to**	(U9)	recover **from**	(U14)
approve **of**	(U2)	rush **through**	(U22)
arrive / be **on** time	(U18)	sense **of** humour	(U2)
at risk **of**	(U5)	shout **at**	(U2)
contribute **to**	(U5)	spend money **on**	(U2)
depend **on**	(U5)	spread **to**	(U9)
do research **on**	(U14)	take advantage **of**	(U9)
dream **of**	(U9)	take part **in**	(U9)
drop **by**	(U14)	vote **for**	(U22)
find a solution **to**	(U18)	work **on**	(U5)
focus **on**	(U5)	work **with**	(U22)
for fun	(U2)		
hold something **by**	(U14)		

Collocations and expressions

a part-time job	(U17)	hand in your notice	(U17)
(be) a natural	(U1)	hang out	(U1)
(be) against the law	(U21)	have a lot in common	(U1)
(be) dying to	(U1)	head in the clouds	(U13)
(be in / get into) hot water	(U13)	in management	(U17)
(be) mad about	(U1)	keep in touch with	(U1)
(be) under arrest	(U21)	lease of life	(U6)
(be) under investigation	(U21)	let somebody off	(U21)
break the law	(U21)	make a difference	(U10)
build a business	(U10)	make an impression	(U10)
build confidence	(U10)	on my last legs	(U6)
calm before the storm	(U13)	on the mend	(U6)
criminal record	(U21)	pay a fine	(U21)
do (you) the world of good	(U6)	pick someone's brains	(U6)
down to earth	(U13)	recharge (your) batteries	(U6)
fall out with	(U1)	reject a job offer	(U17)
fit as a fiddle	(U6)	retail experience	(U17)
gain experience	(U10)	solve a case	(U21)
gain understanding	(U10)	steal someone's thunder	(U13)
get on someone's nerves	(U1)	storm clouds gathering	(U13)
get the sack	(U17)	take a rain check	(U13)
get wind of something	(U13)	take on staff	(U17)
give advice	(U10)	under the weather	(U6)
give someone a chance	(U10)	work shifts	(U17)

Word formation

Adjective → adjective

SIMPLE	SIMPLEST	U24

Adjective → noun

CONFIDENT	CONFIDENCE	U20
CURIOUS	CURIOUSITY	U8
DIFFICULT	DIFFICULTY	R2
EASY	EASE	U20
ILL	ILLNESS	U5, R2
INTENSE	INTENSITY	U14
LONELY	LONELINESS	U1
LONG	LENGTH	U24
MODEST	MODESTY	U9
SIMILAR	SIMILARITY	U4, R2

Adjective → opposite adjective

CREDIBLE	INCREDIBLE	U8
LIKELY	UNLIKELY	U3
USUAL	UNUSUAL	U4, U9

Adjective → verb

SOCIAL	SOCIALISE	U5

Adverbs

ACCIDENT	ACCIDENTALLY	U5
BASIC	BASICALLY	U17
CARE	CAREFULLY	R3
DRAMATIC	DRAMATICALLY	U20
EXCLUSIVE	EXCLUSIVELY	U24
FORTUNATE	UNFORTUNATELY	U14
GENERAL	GENERALLY	R2
INCREASE	INCREASINGLY	R5
NATURE	NATURALLY	U2
ORIGIN	ORIGINALLY	U12
SUBSTANCE	SUBSTANTIALLY	R6
SUCCEED	SUCCESSFULLY	U9
SURPRISE	SURPRISINGLY	U20
TRADITION	TRADITIONALLY	U24

Noun → adjective

AMBITION	AMBITIOUS	U9
BEAUTY	BEAUTIFUL	U24
CATASTROPHE	CATASTROPHIC	U14
CENTRE	CENTRAL	R6
CHEER	CHEERFUL	U2
DANGER	DANGEROUS	U16
ECONOMY	ECONOMIC	R3, R5
EFFECT	EFFECTIVE	R6
GENE	GENETIC	U5
GUILT	GUILTY	U22
LEGEND	LEGENDARY	U3
LIFE	LIVING	R2
MASS	MASSIVE	U14
MISERY	MISERABLE	R3
MOUNTAIN	MOUNTAINOUS	U19
MYSTERY	MYSTERIOUS	U3
MYTH	MYTHICAL	U14
NATURE	NATURAL	U16
OPTIMIST	OPTIMISTIC	U8
PASSION	PASSIONATE	U17
PEACE	PEACEFUL	U1
PEACE	PEACEFUL	R6
PERSON	PERSONAL	R5
PRACTICE	PRACTICAL	R6
PSYCHOLOGY	PSYCHOLOGICAL	R5
RIDICULE	RIDICULOUS	U4
SENSE	SENSIBLE	U1
STRESS	STRESSED	U1
STYLE	STYLISH	U24
THOUGHT	THOUGHTFUL	U12
VALUE	VALUABLE	U12
VIOLENCE	VIOLENT	U22
VOLUNTEER	VOLUNTARY	U17
VOLUNTEER	VOLUNTARY	R3
WEALTH	WEALTHY	U9, R5
WIRE	WIRELESS	U8

Noun → noun

ARCHAEOLOGY	ARCHAEOLOGIST	U3
ARCHITECT	ARCHITECTURE	U19
BREATH	BREATHING	U24
BURGLAR	BURGLARY	U22
CHAMPION	CHAMPION	U2
CRIME	CRIMINAL	U22
ENGINE	ENGINEER	U16
FRIEND	FRIENDSHIP	R3
GYMNAST	GYMNASTICS	U2
JEWEL	JEWELLERY	U24
JOURNAL	JOURNALIST	U16
PERSON	PERSONALITY	U1
POLITICS	POLITICIAN	U16
SCENE	SCENERY	U20
VANDAL	VANDALISM	U22

Noun → verb

EXAM	EXAMINE	U5
PROOF	PROVE	R3

Prefixes

AVOID	UNAVOIDABLE	R2
COURAGE	ENCOURAGE	U8
POPULATE	OVERPOPULATED	U3

Verb → adjective

ATTRACT	ATTRACTIVE	U1, U7
BOARD	BOARDING	U19
CARE	CARING	U2
CHALLENGE	CHALLENGING	U17
CONNECT	CONNECTED	U7
CREATE	CREATIVE	U7, R5
DESTROY	DESTRUCTIVE	U14
DETERMINE	DETERMINED	U9
EMBARRASS	EMBARRASSED	U2
EMPLOY	SELF-EMPLOYED	U17
HELP	HELPFUL	U20
IMAGINE	IMAGINATIVE	U1
IMPRESS	IMPRESSIVE	U20
INSPIRE	INSPIRING	U7
INSPIRE	INSPIRATIONAL	U7
ORGANISE	ORGANISED	U7
QUALIFY	QUALIFIED	U17
REMARK	REMARKABLE	U4, R6
REPEAT	REPETITIVE	U12
RESIST	RESISTANT	U14
REWARD	REWARDING	U17
STICK	STICKY	U4

Verb → noun

ACCOMMODATE	ACCOMMODATION	U19
ACHIEVE	ACHIEVEMENT	U9
ACT	ACTION	U16
ANALYSE	ANALYSIS	U10
APPEAR	APPEARANCE	U3
ASTONISH	ASTONISHMENT	R6
BEHAVE	BEHAVIOUR	U22
CALCULATE	CALCULATOR	U8
CELEBRATE	CELEBRATION	U9
CHOOSE	CHOICE	U20
COLLECT	COLLECTION	U24
COMBINE	COMBINATION	U17
COMPETE	COMPETITION	U7
CONCLUDE	CONCLUSION	U4, U12
CONSUME	CONSUMPTION	U5
DEPART	DEPARTURE	U19
DEPRESS	DEPRESSION	R2
DETERMINE	DETERMINATION	R3
DEVELOP	DEVELOPMENT	U8, R3
DEVELOP	DEVELOPMENT	R6
DISCOVER	DISCOVERY	U4
DONATE	DONATION	R5
EDUCATE	EDUCATION	U2
ENTER	ENTRANCE	U22
ENTHUSE	ENTHUSIASM	U1
ERUPT	ERUPTION	U14
EXPLAIN	EXPLANATION	U4
EXPLODE	EXPLOSION	U7
INHABIT	INHABITANT	R6
INSTRUCT	INSTRUCTOR	U5
INVENT	INVENTION	U7
INVESTIGATE	INVESTIGATION	U3
KNOW	KNOWLEDGE	R3
LAND	LANDING	U19
OBLIGE	OBLIGATION	R5
OPERATE	OPERATOR	U16
PERMIT	PERMISSION	U19
PRESS	PRESSURE	U5
PROVE	PROOF	U12
RECOVER	RECOVERY	R3
RESEARCH	RESEARCHER	U8, U10
RESIDE	RESIDENTS	U4
SETTLE	SETTLEMENT	U3
SITUATE	SITUATION	U4
SOLVE	SOLUTION	U16, R2
TOUR	TOURIST	U19
TRANSLATE	TRANSLATION	U20
VARY	VARIETY	U22

NATIONAL GEOGRAPHIC LEARNING

National Geographic Learning,
a Cengage Company

New Close-up English in Use B1+ Student's Book,
Second Edition
Author: Philip James

Additional material: Helen Kidd

Program Director: Sharon Jervis

Editorial Manager: Claire Merchant

Project Manager: Adele Moss

Head of Strategic Marketing: Charlotte Ellis

Head of Production and Design: Celia Jones

Content Project Manager: Nick Lowe

Manufacturing Manager: Eyvett Davis

Cover Design: Geoff Ward

Compositors: Jonathan Bargus & Elisabeth Heissler
  Graphic Design

Student's Edition:
ISBN: 978-1-473-78638-7

National Geographic Learning
Cheriton House, North Way,
Andover, Hampshire, SP10 5BE
United Kingdom

Locate your local office at **international.cengage.com/region**

Visit National Geographic Learning online at **ELTNGL.com**
Visit our corporate website at **www.cengage.com**

CREDITS

Photos: 5 Adam Smigielski/E+/Getty Images; **9** Sorin Rechitan/EyeEm/Getty Images; **10** Efrain Padro/Alamy Stock Photo; **15** Peter Dazeley/Photodisc/Getty Images; **17** Rowan Romeyn/Alamy Stock Photo; **19** AHMET YARALI/iStockphoto; **23** Miroslav Posavec/Alamy Stock Photo; **34** Jack Andersen/Stone/Getty Images; **42** ipopba/iStockphoto; **47** Izabela Habur/E+/Getty Images; **52** susan.k./Moment/Getty Images; **57** Daisy Daisy/Shutterstock; **60** Imgorthand/E+/Getty Images; **62** Microgen/Shutterstock; **68** Monkey Business Images/Shutterstock; **77** DieterMeyrl/E+/Getty Images; **82** FluxFactory/E+/Getty Images; **87** Westend61/Getty Images; **91** metamorworks/iStockphoto; **95** SDI Productions/iStockphoto; **106** TARIK KIZILKAYA/E+/Getty Images; **111** De Visu/Shutterstock; **116** Mark Bolton Photography/Alamy Stock Photo; **128** Milan Markovic/E+/Getty Images; **132** Inside Creative House/Shutterstock; **136** Richard Newstead/Moment/Getty Images; **138** Maskot/DigitalVision/Getty Images.

ON THE COVER

The cover image shows the Guggenheim Museum in Bilbao, Spain. It was designed by Frank Gehry, a famous architect, and is one of the most famous modern buildings in the world. The museum is so beautiful that millions of visitors have come to Bilbao to see it!
© Kristoff Bellens/Alamy

Printed in Greece by Bakis, SA
Print Number: 01   Print Year: 2022

FSC
MIX
Paper from responsible sources
FSC® C169932